PRAISE FOR *THROUGH* THE CLOSET DOOR

So warm a read! Touching, so funny at times – perfectly juxtaposing emotions. A truly sensational tale of the life of a vivacious, talented person encountering the slings and arrows awaiting her, yet rising phoenix-like from the ashes with undaunted spirit. Heartwarming, tear-jerking, hysterical, and truly written from the heart to you, the reader.

Laura Cross, Founder of Laura Cross Speech and Language Center

One woman's journey along an all too familiar path, discovering the difference between what she's been told and taught by loved ones... to knowing the truth.

Ashley Ashmore

This book is a journey of an older lesbian couple who are loved by family and friends and who, in spite of struggles along the way, wouldn't change a thing.

Tracy Herrera

An inspiring story of transformation.

M. J. Sewall

A brave and honest account that explores deeply personal and difficult topics. A timely memoir perfect for the LGBTQ+ community and those who love and support them.

Angie Torres

I have known Barbara Wilson for 39 years, almost as long as she has been with her wife Sandra. Barb and Sandra are one of the most loving couples I have ever met. Their love for each other is subtle at first glance, but the way they care for each other is profound and evidenced in all their actions. Barb writes with such honesty and clarity about her story that I can't help but feel inspired.

Cuca Silva

THROUGH THE CLOSET DOOR
PART TWO

By

Barbara Wilson

Sound on Sound Publishing

BARBARA WILSON

Sound on Sound Publishing
Santa Maria, CA

Sound on Sound Publishing
Santa Maria, CA

ISBN 13: 979-8-9990987-2-6 *(sc)*

Sound on Sound Publishing, Santa Maria, CA

Book Jacket and Page Design: Matthew J. Pallamary/San Diego CA
Cover artwork: Matthew J. Pallamary/San Diego CA
Author's Photograph: Sandra Wilson/Santa Maria CA

Through The Closet Door
Part Two

BARBARA WILSON

TABLE OF CONTENTS

INTRODUCTION

In the 1960s Midwest, Barbara Wilson is an enthusiastic music director at her Catholic Church on Eastern Michigan University's campus. In addition to her religious teachings, both her parents reinforced the importance of honesty and integrity above all else. When she reports a close friend suspected of lesbianism, the girl is expelled and Barbara feels conflicted.

Two decades later on California's Central Coast, Barbara is the beloved "Miss Wilson" of a special education classroom. Then her neighbor, an unapologetic lesbian, challenges every rule Barbara once preached. Years later, Barbara falls in love with Sandra, a fellow teacher and married mother of three.

On a moonlit night, with the moon eclipsing, a fearful Barbara confesses to Sandra that she is gay. Sandra whispers, "I don't know if I'm gay-I just know I love you." Their clandestine romance must survive small town gossip, religious convictions, family rejection, and the very real threat of losing their jobs.

Even though their love for their grandchildren is equal, the family calls Sandra Nana and Barbara by the name everyone calls her. She can't be Nana Barbs for fear it would cause people to wonder if they are two moms.

Part love story, part spiritual reckoning, Through the Closet Door is an uplifting testament to the freedom that arrives when you refuse to call your love a sin.

ONE

Believe it or Not
Believe it or Not

1995 (Age 47)

Sandra and I were on an annual gambling trip to Laughlin, NV with Mark, Ron, and Fran Brannon, when Sandra came over to me and said, "My parents are right over there."

"No way! Impossible!" The last time we saw Sandra's parents was seven years earlier when her mother slapped Sandra and yelled at me, "You will never be part of my family," before she had a breakdown so serious we almost called an ambulance. Because of their behavior and the fact they had disowned us, we didn't know how they would react to seeing us now. We looked for Mark, Ron, and Fran to tell them, "Sandra's parents are right over there and we're not sure how they will react to seeing us."

"What an amazing coincidence," Ron said. "Let's go meet them."

With Mark's wheelchair leading the way we headed one aisle over to the slot machine her dad, Joe, was playing. He looked up surprised. "How did you know we were here?" he asked Sandra. Her mother heard the commotion and came over. "We didn't know," Sandra answered.

The greeting was tense, even with Ron and Fran and Mark there. Everyone was cordial and surprised that we ended up at the same place at the same time, but nothing changed after that. I wanted to say, "Should we meet for dinner?" It seemed so meant to be, but it wasn't my place to extend a hand. That would have had to come from Joe and Marilyn who didn't take the opportunity to mend the broken fence.

We never saw them again. I thought maybe after they got home from that unbelievable coincidence, they might contact Sandra or the boys, but they never even said, "Good-bye."

I reacted to a man's Facebook Post about the Bible and homosexuality that said, "It is the living word of God and God will not be mocked."

I responded to his long rant about the sanctity of marriage with, "Who wrote the Bible?" Men, throughout the ages who claimed to be messengers of God as it suited their "platform" and their need to be right. If the man who posted the rant actually read the Bible he would realize there are passages that make no sense today, but I doubt he read those. Someone had to be helping him pick and choose bible verses that suited his personality.

In 1946, a committee of men, not God, changed words in the Bible to make homosexuality a sin, so they could be right, and men like the ranter could be right.

I listed other Bible verses below that this man has probably never read, or he would know not to rant, because that's in the Bible too.

I am family after all
Love conquers fear

Several months after ignoring us in Laughlin, Sandra's dad was in his front yard thinning cacti when he became ill. Marilyn called his doctor who advised her to have Joe stay in bed until he got better, but Joe became worse, so she took him to emergency where he was admitted to the hospital. Marilyn got a call from his doctor asking, "Who authorized you to take him to the hospital?"

It's a good thing she did because the doctors at Lompoc Hospital recognized that Joe was having a stroke. Unbeknownst to Sandra, her Dad was in Lompoc Hospital getting worse and worse for three days, after which they sent Joe to Santa Barbara.

Sandra's mother finally called Sandra at school, and as soon as her students left Sandra headed to Martha Negus to pick me up. The minute I saw her face I asked, "What's wrong?"

"Dad's in a hospital in Santa Barbara. That's all I know."

We drove from Martha Negus to Marilyn's home in Lompoc where Marilyn described Joe's condition as terrifying. "He was unresponsive."

Sandra found the paperwork with the name and address of the facility Joe was in. We put Marilyn in the back seat and headed for Santa Barbara while Marilyn talked non-stop. The fact she was in the presence of two lesbians seemed irrelevant. Sandra gave me directions to the facility, and I dropped the two of them off at the front door and parked the car. I became nauseous from the smell of urine when I entered the building. It permeated the entire building and the atmosphere was chaotic without one calm staff person anywhere. I stopped someone with a name tag on her blouse. "Is there any rehab here for stroke victims?"

"No," she answered, annoyed that I had interrupted her.

I found the room where Marilyn, Sandra and Joe were. He looked comatose lying fully dressed on top of his bed with a dark stain revealing he had wet himself, totally unaware of his pathetic condition. Sandra pointed out that he was so out of it he wouldn't be able to operate a call button which was a moot point. She had pushed it ten minutes earlier and nobody responded.

There was no way Joe was going to remain in that pit. No way!

"This place shouldn't even be in business," we agreed. Sandra and I told Marilyn we were getting Joe out of there and prayed they would have room for him at the Santa Barbara Rehabilitation Center.

We drove to the Santa Barbara Rehab Center and our prayers were answered when they arranged for Joe to be picked up and transferred to SBRC that very minute. We went back and told Marilyn and waited by his side until the ambulance arrived and transferred Joe out of the pit. He wasn't even aware he was being transferred. I drove the three of us to SBRC, and it was like night and day compared to the pit. We were directed to a calm office with a professional woman at a quiet desk. Joe was going to get intensive daily therapy and great care.

During those months Joe was in rehab we drove Marilyn for an hour to visit him every day after we had been teaching all day on weekdays and every weekend. Marilyn was grateful and knew I had played a big part in getting Joe into SBRC. She also got to know me because after we spent time with Joe, we went out for dinner in Santa Barbara before heading home. Marilyn finally ended up liking me, realizing that I was indeed family.

When we first visited Joe at the SBRC, he was non-functioning and hallucinating about being in the war. I didn't have much hope for him to recover, but he came out of there a couple of months later cured except for needing a cane to help him walk.

Unbelievable.

After Joe "graduated" from SBRC, Sandra and I started picking him and Marilyn up one day a week to drive them to the Chumash Casino, a half hour away from their house. We had dinner at a family-owned restaurant in Buellton and chatted during dinner. Once we were at the casino everyone went their separate ways.

My mother was happy Joe and Marilyn finally accepted Sandra and me. On weekends, we had everyone to our house for dinner and Texas Hold 'em. Everyone got along and appreciated our invitation. Sandra was hostess extraordinaire and mom didn't drink too much with them because Sandra's parents didn't drink. Mom hated going to the casino because she couldn't stand losing money, even when it was money I gave her. "This is money I've saved just for gambling, mom." She didn't enjoy it like the rest of us. There was no fun in gambling even though we bet the least amount possible. In her mind getting to spend time with us wasn't worth the foolhardiness of gambling.

"If you know you're going to lose, why do you do it? "she said rolling her eyes.

"Because it's fun when you win, mom, and I can afford to lose. I consider it entertainment."

I must have gone from devil to saint in Joe's mind. He thanked me for taking care of Sandra and told me I was the best thing that ever happened to her. I told him that it worked both ways. She was the best thing that ever happened to me. I always qualified that with an acknowledgement that I had very devoted parents, so meeting Sandra tied as the best thing that ever happened to me.

Marilyn changed her mind about me, too. Whenever we were out she introduced me as family. In fact she was more "out" about my relationship with Sandra than I was. I forgave her for all those years of disowning us and her grandchildren.

Their example didn't help the general public, but they were living Jesus's message. Be a good person and respect those who deserve respect.

Nov. 4, 1998, Bailey

It was a nice change to be spending more time with our parents and an even nicer change was the birth of our first grandchild. Sandra's youngest son Jon and his wife Melinda gave birth to Bailey which gave Melinda's son Hayze a half-sister. We looked forward to every minute with Bailey who was pure joy. I didn't have her call me Gramma, or Nana Barbs, or anything else that indicated Sandra and I were a couple. Jon and Melinda seemed to be excellent parents.

Jason returned from his job as a butcher in Colorado Springs where he was an expert fisherman and loved the outdoors. He and Jon worked for Smith Electric, a company owned by our friends the Brannon's. Jon got a very prestigious award, and we took Bailey on an overnight trip to see him get it which was impressive, and it was nice to spend the weekend with him and Melinda.

Justin stayed busy twenty four hours a day with Apollo Enterprises where he was CEO along with two of his buddies. The company kept growing, creating websites for Warner Brothers, Jack in the Box, the Gap, nine casinos, and much more. Sandra and I always checked his website saying, "Hey, look at this. Oh my God."

OK, the truth is that I say, "Oh my God," because my God has bigger things to worry about than people saying, "Oh my God," and who says we shouldn't say "Oh my God?" Leviticus 24:10-16.

If I say the F word, shit, or damn it, I am upset and cursing. When I say, "Oh my God," It's in wonderment, not cursing, so for this biblical take it or leave it, I leave it – a lot.

TWO

Sound on Sound

When Sandra and I became a couple I sang every Saturday outside a group of stores and restaurants in Solvang. Sandra came with me, but I couldn't get her to sing. "You have a great voice." I told her.

"No, I don't, I have a horrible voice. People have told me."

"Well, the people are wrong," I said, but she didn't believe me.

If I took a bathroom break, she played DJ instead of singing while I was gone.

She finally sang some duets with me, and after months of compliments from me and strangers, sang the melodies while I did harmonies. Our voices blended so well you couldn't tell who sang what part. All of our gigs were for heterosexual events until we got a call to sing the last weekend in June in Malibu at a women's weekend at Camp Shalom, and What a weekend. It was the first time Sandra and I had been to an all woman event, but I couldn't even say "lesbians" back then. It was one of the coolest weekends of our life. There were lectures, games, and a dance. It was so cool watching the women dance to our music, and this dance was our "in" to other women's dances and parties and events.

We were particularly busy the weekend of the Dinah Shore golf tournament in Rancho Mirage. We entertained at the "Never Too Old to Party" on the Friday nights until several members passed away and it was too sad to party without them. Sandra and I stayed at Dorothey Reed's house for that weekend and did her annual dance for four hours on her patio on Sunday while watching gay men and women dance to our music.

Dorothey sadly passed away and will be missed when that weekend comes around. We also played for private parties that weekend. Sandra loved attending the golf tournament thanks to our friends Jane and Diane who gave her tickets every year. We also played for "The Women's Company" parties for several years and for private birthday parties in Palm Springs which led to our New Year's Eve parties in Apache Junction; The Pueblo, and Superstition Mountain; both 55+ Women's Communities, where we were introduced to pickleball. We also got invited to couples' homes to watch the New Years Day football games and eat all day with other women. I say we "did" those parties, but I'm still as active and capable as ever to drive to Palm Springs or elsewhere for gigs.

Locally Dr. Pat Brenner became a best friend because of her parties in Arroyo Grande and Palm Springs. She was a blessing to us in every way and we were always welcome to stay at her house when we were in the area. She wrote a book entitled "The Conscious Mind" that is quite interesting.

We've also entertained at Celebrity Cruises; a convention at the Golden Nugget; Yacht Club-Long Beach; Hyatt Regency-Hollywood; Sun Lakes CC-Banning; Sun City-Palm Desert; 7 Lakes CC-Palm Springs; Palm Desert Greens CC; Torrey Pines CC; Homestead in Orcutt; Laetitia and Kula wineries, and Dell Webb communities.

I hope this book sparks interest in hiring me. I feel like I am better than ever because I continue to practice and learn new songs. Sandra has retired from small events but says she will help when I need her.

THREE

The Eve of Destruction
1999-2000 Hysteria to the max. Nothing will work - psych!

What was originally referred to as CDC, Century Data Change, became known as Y2K and it wasn't just fanatics creating hysteria. Here's what the U.S. Secretary of Defense sent out:

"The Y2K problem is the electronic equivalent of the El Niño and there will be nasty surprises around the globe." The New York Times wrote, "This is the information age equivalent of the midnight ride of Paul Revere."

The Y2K bug was a computer flaw predicted to cause problems when dealing with dates beyond December 31,1999. When computer programs were written in the 1960s through 1980s engineers used a two-digit code for the year, leaving the "19" out. The fear was that computers would treat 00 as 1900 instead of 2000. By 1997 AT&T estimated that 60% of the time and money needed for compliance would be devoted to addressing the Y2K issue. I never understood what all that meant, but I knew we were likely headed for a serious problem. They predicted that every computer in the world would crash, which meant elevators would stop, credit cards and ATM's would stop functioning, and trains and planes wouldn't operate. Ten percent of the population believed it was an apocalypse. Others believed it was the second coming of Christ. Gun sales soared, and fear and hysteria ran rampant. It was Covid-19 stress times ten. They feared we would lose every piece of technology available to us. Folks like me who don't ordinarily become unreasonably fearful became fearful enough to take cash out of my bank account. Some people took all

17

their money out making people like me think, "What if they are right?" Most of us couldn't explain the specifics of the problem, we just knew that anything digital wasn't ready to handle turning over to 2000.

Sandra and I were hired to bring in 2000 at the Village Country Club near Lompoc where we had been hired many times before and were happy to be amongst friends if all the lights went out or whatever unforeseeable event occurred.

We drove for half an hour to the club to set up that afternoon and returned later dressed up and ready to play for our 9:00 start. We went around and asked for requests and took bets on whether the clock was going to turn to 12:00 at midnight. Most people didn't want to guess. Some had already checked with different time zones and remained secretive. We had so many requests we started before 9:00.

Our audience clapped and danced to every song we played. Sandra lined up their requests during times she didn't sing and we kept reminding people we were celebrating the most important New Year's Eve of all time. "No more writing checks starting with 19," I reminded the audience. One hour passed. Two hours passed and it was already 11:30. "Half an hour left of 1999," I reminded the audience.

Finally, our clocks approached midnight. "Come on everybody! 10—9—8—7—6—5—4—3—2—1. Happy New Year!" Everyone yelled holding up glasses of champagne, then instead of kissing their spouses while Sandra and I sang Auld Lang Syne, they looked at the clocks and watches cheering louder than ever, then kissing their spouses and hugging everyone more enthusiastically than ever. The clock on the wall said 1-1-2000.

The congratulatory champagne felt more meaningful than ever. We played a six-minute big band medley that got everyone on the floor. Some people admitted they knew ahead of time because of time changes, but most wanted to experience the surprise together.

The following day I heard about an expert who argued that scaremongering occurred. The next day on the same news stations I heard, "Ross Anderson, a professor of security engineering at Cambridge University sent out hundreds of press releases that the problem was NOT likely to be a big problem."

I never heard of Ross Anderson or anyone else who said it might not be a big problem. As our editor Wayne always said, "If it's good news, it's not news."

That professor should have been a featured speaker on every news station in the country, lowering our stress levels, but it was only after the safe turning of the clocks that night that our fears were quelled.

FOUR

Prop 22 3/2000 to 11/2000 - The Knight Initiative - March 2000

MAY 15, 2008 PROP 22 was struck down by the California Supreme Court as contrary to the state constitution. From May 2008 to November 2008 same gender couples could get married and many happily did.

Pete Knight, the author of prop 22 was a Mormon father whose son was his pride and joy, especially when he returned home from the Gulf War. When his son came out as gay his father disowned him with Bible verses to justify his harsh and cruel actions. This man's homophobia combined with his need to be right was stronger than his love for his own son and we all had to pay the price.

Why weren't any of these other sins on the signs in California important? Personally I would have picked NO CRITICIZING, NO HURTING OTHERS, or NO BEING UNETHICAL. Pedophiles are sick sinful people who need to be institutionalized away from children, so please stop confusing two adults who love each other with men who have sex with underage boys. The word homosexual wasn't even in the Bible until a committee of self-righteous men added it in 1946. God didn't add it to the Bible. Men did, telling others they are messengers of God when they were messengers of different people throughout times, often conflicting with each other.

The SAVE MARRIAGE signs were huge and you couldn't turn on the TV without hearing negative propaganda about us. We could never figure out whose marriage would be destroyed if we got married. Their signs may have saved marriages whatever that means, but they destroyed families.

I read an eight page suicide note from a distraught Mormon in his twenties. His family tried to support him, but even their support wasn't enough to counteract the hate and bigotry he felt from his church, and he wasn't alone.

The suicide rate for gay teens is three times higher than their peers. Twenty two percent of gay teens skip school because they fear for their safety. In one college questionnaire eighteen percent of males admitted physically assaulting or threatening people they thought were gay or lesbian while thirty two percent admitted verbally harassing gays and lesbians. Those huge hate filled signs reinforced those kinds of attitudes and behaviors.

Every time I saw one of those huge signs I imagined grandkids asking their parents or grandparents what they meant, and then I tried to imagine how their parents and grandparents answered them. Hopefully, our grandkids would be perplexed as to why anyone would vote against their Nana and Barbara.

The people who agreed with those signs were self-righteous, smugly moralistic, and intolerant.

Fifty years ago, my parents didn't know any better when they taught me about "queers", but people today can't claim to not know any better. It's destructive to individuals and their families. This isn't a family value, it's an anti-family value. Holding on to those harmful archaic values is sinful, belittling, and unethical; all sins, right there in the Bible. I'm sure the church's intent is not rejection and harm, but when you read letters from children from those sects, it breaks your heart. God celebrates diversity not division. I firmly believe that He will be judging me much kinder than those who are so comfortable making such sinful judgements in His name. Their judgement day will come. How could those divisive, ignorant, discriminatory, bigoted signs possibly be pleasing to God?

In February Sandra and I entertained in Palm Springs and someone gave us a NO ON 22 sign. On the way home we discussed putting it in our yard and wondered how our neighbors would react. In Palm Springs most yards had a NO ON 22 sign and we hoped that at least a couple of our neighbors would have a NO ON 22 sign proudly displayed in their yard. After a four hour drive discussing our sign we turned onto our street and got our answer. House after house after house had YES ON 22 signs.

We looked at each other in disbelief. "Can you believe people feel this strongly about us? I can't believe it!" I kept repeating.

"I can't believe it either. Almost every house." Sandra followed up.

"Except ours and we're sure not putting ours out."

"That's for sure. Someone might vandalize our car or house.

"I bet there's not one 'No' sign in all of Santa Maria for fear of a hate crime. What a difference from Palm Springs. This is so upsetting." Sandra finished, disappointed and discouraged.

After a night of closeness and comfort together I told Sandra, "I have to talk to the neighbors. Do you think they don't know we're gay?"

"Beats me." Sandra said. "I haven't got the faintest idea."

"Well I have to find out. I'm baffled and I have to talk to them. I'm going across the street first to find out for both of us."

"You won't change any minds."

"I can't possibly not look into this. Aren't you even curious whether they know about us? What possessed them to put those signs out? Aren't you even curious?"

"Of course I'm curious. You're just gonna have to find out by yourself because I think you're wasting your time, and I'm not going with you."

"I don't mind finding out for both of us because it's driving me crazy. I think they like us, so do they like us and not know we're gay?"

I went across the street and could see Sandra watching me from the kitchen window as I passed the sign on their lawn and knocked on their door. Our neighbor opened it and welcomed me in, inviting me to sit down on their couch while they sat in chairs eager to know why I was visiting. Usually, I went to give them their mail after we tended their mailbox while they were on vacation. I struggled to keep my lip from quivering.

"Would you like anything to drink?" they asked, motioning to their kitchen.

"No thank you. I'm not going to be here for long, but thank you." I took a big breath and continued, "I'm here because of your sign." I hesitated. "Do you realize Sandra and I are a couple?" I stammered.

They leaned toward me. "Someone delivered the signs and we hadn't given much thought to putting it up," they explained. "We really like you and Sandra. We just weren't thinking. We'll take it down."

I left their house and went to the neighbor on their right and stood outside their door for a long time, breathing deep. Finally, I rang their doorbell. Those neighbors were good friends who liked us and we liked them. Their doorbell seemed louder than usual. They both greeted me and stepped aside to direct me to the kitchen table where they offered me some orange juice.

"Yes please." I felt grateful for having something to distract me. We made small talk while I waited for the juice, then I started. "I'm here because I'm surprised you have a Yes on 22 sign on your lawn. I assume you don't realize Sandra and I are a couple?"

I could tell by their faces that I had started an awkward conversation. They stayed silent so I waited for them to speak. They obviously hadn't realized Sandra and I were a couple, then came a real shocker when they shared with me the fact their only son was gay, and no longer in their life. I felt like I was the only person they had ever shared that with. I asked about him and their answers were brief and vague. I got the impression they didn't know where he was, then the conversation became so uncomfortable, I decided to leave without quizzing them further. I couldn't wait to get home and share my news with Sandra.

"Sandra, I'm so glad I talked to everyone. No one knew we were gay, and I think it's good they now know because they like us, and they said they would take their sign down. Now wait 'til you hear this! Their son is gay and estranged from them."

"Wow, that's interesting. Do you think they will call him after your talk?"

"I have no clue. " I responded. I sure hope so, but they gave me no indication they would contact him. I'm not even sure they know where he is."

The next day both signs were removed. I don't know if I changed votes, but Sandra and I appreciated having two fewer signs of disapproval as we drove down our street. I would like to believe my frank and difficult talk with both neighbors helped to educate them and that the neighbor we were close to would reunite with their son. I was worried my talk with them would change their feelings about Sandra and me, but they continued to visit us.

Does God want children disowned? Does God want families destroyed? Does God want depression, suicide, anguish, and siblings who feel they are better than their brother or sister? People who are gender non-conforming feel love from their God, not from their church. Does God want those children who pray to Him not to have their prayers answered? They pray their families will accept them while their families tell them they should be praying to change.

Sandra and I have met hundreds of lesbian couples who are more devoted and respectful to their spouses than heterosexuals are, so I'm sure God was not calling homosexuality sinful. Promiscuity is sinful.

Rape is sinful. Pedophilia is sinful. None of that applies to homosexuality which is about two consenting adults falling in love.

Prop 22 was approved with a polarizing sixty one percent of voters in favor of preventing marriage between same-gender couples. Almost two thirds of Californians were against Sandra and me marrying, and we set an example of what marriage should be, love, commitment, respect, and a promise to be there in good times and in bad, forever. It felt unfair that anyone who was registered to vote had the right to weigh in on our lifestyle. People with anger problems could vote against our gentle and respectful lifestyle. People who were divorced could vote against committed lifestyle. Unhappy people could vote against our happy lifestyle and people who were unfaithful could vote against our commitment. Save marriage? There were plenty of straight marriages that needed saving, but not from us. The irony is that most of those voters were the same ones who screamed about not wanting government interference in their lives; except when it benefitted them. I was inspired to write to Senator Diane Feinstein.

Dear Ms. Feinstein,

My wonderful partner and I have been together for almost 16 years. I can't imagine anyone having a more respectful or deeper love than ours. I don't think being married would change our personal relationship in anyway, but it would make our social life, family life, professional life, and our finances much less complicated. How can we expect society to give us the respect we deserve if our educated leaders don't give us the respect we deserve? To consider our relationship to be less than anyone else's perpetuates a very misguided and harmful prejudice. It's way past time for this injustice to be corrected. I pray that you will use your power to change this injustice and take pride in your courageous and just decision.

I can't describe the hurt I felt driving past a co-worker's house with a NO ON 22 sign on her front lawn. I knew she was Mormon, but I didn't think she felt strongly enough to display a sign that everyone, including me, could see. I felt that it had a detrimental impact on my relationship with her even though I tried to forget about it when I saw her at school, then I wrote her a letter.

You must know how much I like you and feel honored to be your co-worker, so your opinion matters to me. Since you have probably never experienced prejudice, you can't empathize with the extreme hurt I felt when I saw that you put a sign in your yard that indicated your disrespect of my loving relationship with Sandra. From then on, it's been difficult to be with you, knowing you consider me less than you. I guess you could argue that you just feel that way about part of me... But that part of me is me.

If there is a God looking down on us, I can promise you I have no fear of that God judging my relationship with Sandra. When I am at weddings I hear the biblical reading: Love is patient... Love is kind...and I think to myself, "that's us. We set the example. People should be learning from us instead of considering our relationship unworthy of marriage."

I don't know if you are one of the people who says, "If we let gays marry the next thing will be polygamy and pedophilia. Where does it stop? I'll tell you exactly where it stops. It stops with what God says is right. How ignorant can people be? I feel that if you have a private conversation about this with your personal God and not your fallible church and fallible Bible interpretations, your God will lead you to a loving, educated, and non-prejudicial stand on this issue. Frankly. my God finds those signs the epitome of sin.

Sandra and I are not any different from other gay couples. Many of them have been in committed relationships for over thirty years and many have been together for over fifty. Don't they deserve to be married? It is wrong that those relationships are disrespected. God has already blessed their marriage. It was hard looking at those signs because they don't speak for God. They demonstrate ignorance and prejudice, and my God finds them immoral. Churches are wrong about this issue and are causing pain for everyone, especially their own members who have gay children. Everyone has to look at those self-righteous signs.
Sincerely,
Barbara

I never gave it to her because I doubted I would change her mind, and it would have created more tension between us.

More than 34,000 people die by suicide each year and LGBTQ youth attempt four times more than their heterosexual peers.

FIVE

Mom Had a Stroke
Lived with us temporarily

Mom had a stroke and lost her ability to speak. She willingly came to live with us and had a room of her own. She could take care of herself for the most part, but had lost her ability to communicate. Our good friend Laurie Cross from Cross Speech Therapy Center came to see mom, and we were able to get her the best speech therapist possible. I helped design a notebook of pictures for mom, but she had no interest in learning it. I'm sure mom had good reasons because she liked to please and be cooperative, but that notebook prevented her from being either so I gave it up.

I took a couple days off and tried to determine how safe Mom would be when left alone, and after two days I felt that she could be. Her cognition seemed OK. It was mostly her inability to communicate that caused us frustration. I put a big NO above the oven and she understood. I wanted her to be hearing speech as much as possible so I left the TV on all day, but when we got home she was almost always out in the back yard choosing the silence of the fields to the noise of the TV.

With the exception of her insistence on not using the notebook to communicate, mom was as easy going as one could expect, considering what she had been through. She was no problem for us to have at home, but we knew she preferred being in her own home. Sandra was amazing at figuring out what Mom was trying to communicate while I got frustrated trying to guess what mom was saying. Sandra would kindly interfere saying, "She wants to…" and Mom would laugh with delight.

Mom already had her flight booked to visit Phyllis at Lake Anna Virginia. Phyllis was happy to have her, but we had to make sure there were no problems with the flight so we booked a nonstop. I drove Mom to her house, and she knew where her suitcase was, and sure enough it was packed and ready to go. Mom always packed months before any trip.

The day of the trip we drove her four hours from Santa Maria to LAX and got her checked in as disabled. We were able to stay with her right up until she boarded and watch her board with an assistant. I called Phyllis. "Mom's on the plane."

Everyone prayed. Mom would be on that plane unable to communicate for over five hours.

Sandra and I headed home and stopped to eat. Shortly after we got home Phyllis called to say "Mom's here!"

SIX

Mom's Caregivers
Became our Lesbian Friends

I figured while mom was at Phyllis's I had six weeks to find someone to move in with her to make sure she was safe. She found cooking confusing but could cook with help. Since she lived a few miles from Hancock College, my first thought was that a couple of students could live with her.

With that thought in the back of my head, Sound on Sound entertained at the grand opening of Santa Maria's LGBT Center. After the gig three of us couples went out for dinner. One couple was new to the area and were staying in a hotel. They were moving to the area because one of their daughter's was a teacher in Lompoc. Her job had something to do with healthcare and Medicare, and her partner had been a caregiver for her own mother before she passed away. We talked and shared quite a bit about ourselves and left the diner without exchanging phone numbers.

The next day we while sitting in a parking lot, I said to Sandra, "I wish I had asked those ladies for their phone number so I could talk with them about moving in with mom. They said they were living in a hotel. Stupid. Stupid! Stupid!" I yelled louder and louder. The one said she took care of her mom. Why didn't I get their number? They might be perfect. I'll go to Hancock tomorrow.

Believe it or not, as we sat with me getting more upset, we saw the two ladies walking into Home Depot where we were headed.

"Hey look!" I said to Sandra. "Isn't that the two ladies we had dinner with? The ladies we are looking for?"

What were the chances? Home Depot! They were living in a hotel and they were headed to Home Depot? We jumped out of the car and ran to catch up with them.

They couldn't believe the coincidence either. I asked if they could join us for lunch to discuss the possibility of them moving out of their hotel and moving into mom's three-bedroom home. This was fate all around. A win-win.

I called Phyllis to tell her I had found two women and the one already knew how to get SSI, so we decided they would live with mom rent free and get paid SSI.

When Mom's visit with Phyllis was over we planned for Phyllis to fly with mom to Las Vegas where we all met. We told the care givers how grateful we were to find them and meant it. We flew back home, and Phyllis flew back to Virginia, agreeing these ladies seemed like a good match for Mom's situation. Thank you, God.

As Sandra and I grew to know them better they became one more lesbian couple we considered friends. They were both nice and interesting. One of them was brilliant and knew about anything and everything. She was the brains, and her partner was more responsible for Mom's physical needs.

Sandra and I brought mom to our house on Saturday afternoons through Sunday night so she could spend a night with us and give her caregivers a break. During those times I asked Mom if everything was ok. Her yes and no answers couldn't be trusted, but I could tell from her facial expressions that she preferred the caregiver that physically helped her. We also had Sandra's parents over on weekends to play games that mom could play. Our other friends had parties on weekends and always included Mom because they knew she was with us on weekends. I would take our karaoke system, and mom would sing "Unchained Melody," bringing tears to everyone's eyes. She couldn't pronounce the words to the song right, but she belted out the melody and loved being the hit of the party.

After a couple of months mom's caregivers asked if they could move their dad in. We had no problem with that and mom said "Yes" too. It didn't take away from her care, and it gave her company her own age, but he was only there for a couple of months before he passed away.

Mom's income was $400 a month and her house payment was $200. She was a super saver and wasn't a shopper. She was the thriftiest person I knew. I was always impressed with how she could make so little go so far. Phyllis and I gave her extra money, and she always saved that for travel to Phyllis's house. Because mom had so little monthly income, I was comfortable giving her caregivers her bank account information to pay the mortgage and utilities, knowing that if they were dishonest, there wasn't anything for them to steal, and fortunately they weren't dishonest.

SEVEN

A Criminal Investigation

Sandra and I were on our way to visit mom on a weekday when a lady walked up to her house at the same time we did with a big envelope in her hand. She said she was looking for Carolyn Wilson and I told her that my mother had a stroke, and I was her daughter, so she could give whatever she had for mom to me. Instead of going into the house Sandra and I went back to our car and opened the envelope there.

"Oh shit!! Shit! Shit!" I screamed. "I can't believe this! Look at this, Sandra. Read it!"

"I can't believe it either," Sandra choked out. Mom's mortgage payment was in arrears. "There must be some mistake," I said. Our good lesbian friends wouldn't let that happen to us and Mom, would they?

My entire body felt weak as we went into Mom's house to talk to the caregivers. Mom was in her bedroom when I showed the envelope to the caregiver in charge of paperwork and asked her how it happened. "It must have gotten in arrears when my dad died, and I had so much going on," she said calmly.

That sounded reasonable since the paperwork didn't say how many months the payment was in arrears; just that it was in arrears. Sandra and I left, still pleased with Mom's caregivers.

"It would make sense they forgot to send in a payment when she was dealing with her dad's death," I said when we were back in the car.

Sandra agreed. "But make sure you call the mortgage company."

"Of course, I'll call the mortgage company!"

As soon as we got home I called the mortgage company and hung up screaming, "The house is being foreclosed in five days if a payment isn't received immediately. In five days!" I screamed louder. "I can't believe this! Sandra, can you? Can you imagine if Mom knew this? She never missed a payment and now her house is five days from

31

foreclosing? If we hadn't been walking to her house the same moment that lady was, we never would have known. My heart was in my throat.

I sat down with the bill and paid everything that was owed on the house and more, insuring that it couldn't happen again, then for the first time I researched Mom's caregivers with a high end research program. When I typed in the smart one's name my stomach turned and I was about to throw up. "Sandra come look at this." One had been in jail for Medical-care fraud!

Here's one article we found; a criminal investigation from the early 1990's provides another example of how vulnerable the Federal healthcare programs are to the schemes of dishonest billing companies. In this case two sisters set up a third-party billing company to perform charge audits for nursing homes. The two sisters persuaded at least 70 nursing homes in eight states that they would review residence medical records and account for services that had not been billed to Medicare. Using tricks of the trade known only to them the company billed Medicare on behalf of the nursing home for these overlooked charges and kept 50% of the proceeds. In actuality the company billed for surgical dressings for nursing home patients who had not had surgery and fraudulently caused Medicare to pay approximately $7.4 million in non-rendered services.

Because the billing company submitted the fraudulent claims under the nursing homes provider number, it took the OIG investigators a great deal of time and resources to tie what appeared to be unrelated improper billing by different nursing homes back to a single third-party billing company. At the conclusion of the investigation the two sisters were convicted of Medicare fraud and received prison sentences.

I couldn't breathe. Tell me this was a dream because one of those sisters was living in my mother's house along with her lesbian partner. I couldn't leave my chair. "A criminal investigation from the 1990's. A criminal investigation from the 1990's." I kept reading it over and over again, and every time I read it I felt sicker. It was the most stressed I'd ever been in my life. What was I going to tell Phyllis?

EIGHT

Mom Died on my Watch
She was so loved by so many

November 4th
The first thing we did was move mom in with us while we continued researching the women who were still living in mom's house without her there. Every day we found new depressing discoveries about them, then mom fell getting into our car. I picked her up and managed to get her into the car by myself, but she couldn't talk because of her stroke. She was trying to communicate she was okay and didn't seem hurt.

"Oh mom, I am so sorry you fell. I'm taking you to emergency."

"No, no, no," she said, one of the only words she was capable of saying.

"You might have hit your head or done something serious I can't see. It's just to be on the safe side. I ran into the house, grabbed my purse and told Sandra, "I'm taking mom to emergency. She seems okay but I just want to make sure.

"I'll go with you."

They put Mom in a room so she could lie down, and she and Sandra waited while I signed mom in at the front desk. By the time I got back to her bed I expected to hear we'd be taking her home.

"They're admitting her to the hospital" Sandra said quietly.

"No Way," I whispered.

We stayed with Mom while they took her upstairs and watched them attach a breathing tube to her. She was lying quietly and I kept talking to her, trying to comfort her but she grew quieter and quieter.

Sandra went downstairs and brought us food and ice cream for mom who didn't respond to the ice cream. Sandra and I moved two chairs by her bed and held her hand. "How are you feeling Mom?" I asked.

She didn't respond.

I leaned over and kissed her. "I love you Mom," I repeated that over and over as I held her hand.

A different doctor came in and examined mom, then called Sandra and I aside. "Your mother is dying," he told us.

I didn't cry because I didn't believe him. "No way! That's not possible. She just walked to my car. She can't be dying."

He explained how he knew, but I didn't hear any of it because my brain shut down. Aspiration Pneumonia was mentioned, but mom looked more alive than the dozens of times I thought she was dead in bed at our house.

I continued telling mom how much I loved her and thought, I'd better call Phyllis, who broke down on the phone. "We will be there as soon as possible." It was going to take her hours, but they were leaving immediately.

I called Cathy Cook at VTC and let her know Mom wouldn't be showing up to volunteer on Monday because she was dying. Cathy was close to Mom.

"What room is she in?" she asked.

"412."

"I'll be right there."

The staff from VTC came to Mom's hospital room and I became upset because I wanted mom to die peacefully, but it turned out to be the best thing that could've happened. We sang for Mom and each of them held her hand. I got to hear them tell mom how much she meant to them and how loved she was by each client. They told her what a difference she made in so many lives. I hadn't heard any of those stories. She got to hear that we were going to have her memorial service at VTC and how crowded it would be because she had touched so many lives.

After everyone left I kept praying that Phyllis and her family would make it. Sandra and I both cried and sang all night to her, including our traditional "Toora Loora Loora" which I had learned from Mom's Dad, Grampa. After all the friends left, Sandra and I just continued holding mom's hand. The only way we knew she was still alive was when she pulled the oxygen tube out of her nose, and I wondered if I should go against her wishes and put it back in hoping to keep her alive until Phyllis got there. Sandra and I fell asleep sitting in chairs beside mom's bed leaned over with our heads on her bed, both of us holding mom's hand. Unlike Joe, I never heard her take her last breath. The nurse told us it was over at 5 am, and we were still holding her hand. I felt indescribably lonely, empty, sad, and in a stupor. Nothing mattered. I took Mom's Timex watch off and swore I would wear it forever. It was hard to leave her alone in the hospital bed. When we had Mom every weekend there were hundreds of times I stared at her thinking she was dead, but none of that prepared me for her real passing. I should have been more prepared, but I wasn't. There is no pain like the pain of losing someone.

While Mom was dying I called Leslie in Palm Springs and said, "I'm sorry Leslie, but I can't do your party, my mother is dying."

"You will be at my party. We have a contract. You will be at my party," she repeated in a voice I didn't dare dispute.

I couldn't believe my ears. The emotions I felt were indescribable, but mostly, "How am I going to tell Phyllis, who was flying out from Maryland. We had a funeral to plan and an estate to discuss, and I had to tell Phyllis I was entertaining five hours away while she was there for Mom's funeral. How would I get through a party?

Phyllis and her family made it the following morning and we planned Mom's celebration. Her son Don helped me with the slide show and Sandra and I left for Palm Springs the day of Leslie's party. I cried the entire way there, but when we got to Leslie's house and set up I didn't shed one tear even though I deeply resented every moment I was there. No one would have known my mother died the day before. Sandra was careful to avoid songs like, Wind Beneath My Wings and Snowbird. I felt guilty about doing the job, but kept rationalizing that Mom knew I had no choice.

We stayed overnight in a hotel, though I couldn't sleep with thoughts running through my head. I was relieved when morning arrived and Sandra drove us back to meet with Phyllis about Mom's estate. Phyllis and her family stayed at our house because Mom's house was occupied by thieves.

Mom died on Bailey's fifth birthday, another nice coincidence in our life.

NINE

The stress never stopped
It was unending "I Can't Believe This is Happening."

My sister's family went home after Mom's funeral and Sandra and I went to the police with a $6875 bill on a credit card I had torn up when Mom had her stroke. Not only were they not paying Mom's mortgage, the credit card company said they wanted payment on my mother's card. I told them I wasn't going to pay it and the people using it had stolen my mother's identity. A Santa Maria detective talked to a detective where they had previously lived, and he said he was glad they were no longer his jurisdiction.

The Santa Maria detective wanted to search mom's house to see if there were any other credit cards, possible crimes, or evidence he needed to research them further. He arrested them and searched mom's house where he found paperwork from my mother's neighbor with her social security number on it. He also found a $3700 eBay bill, a $1400 United Parcel bill, and a $133 book club bill in my mother's name.

My stomach wrenched.

I the thieving women a month's notice to vacate Mom's house and in in an unimaginable act of hubris, the women who stole my mother's identity while living rent free in her house that I was paying for were suing *me*!

I never had a lawyer in my life and suddenly I had three, a criminal lawyer because they had stolen my mother's identity, an estate lawyer because when my mother died I needed to know where all this fit into her estate versus mine, and now I had a lawyer to fight their lawsuit against me. Three lawyers because these sociopaths lied, saying I owed them money for the extra hours they claimed to work beyond what Medicare paid them and claimed it was over $60,000.

My stomach felt queasy and I wanted to barf.

Prior to this incident I believed that no matter what was happening in my students' homes, they should be able to pay attention in school. Now *I* couldn't pay attention in school or anywhere else. My every thought and conversation was about these two criminals. I was already stressed and perplexed with the pain and sorrow of losing my mother. How could this happen?

When the next month rolled around and they were still in my mother's house I arranged for the police to serve them a legal paper that said they had to vacate, and they told the policeman I was harassing them by calling them forty times a day! I had dialed my mother's easy number every day and I dialed it by mistake once, hanging up before they even answered. The last thing I wanted in my life was hearing either of their voices, even once.

I sat at my computer all day researching them and emailing my Santa Barbara lawyer every night with updates. I found out more about them, and he kept telling me that 90% of these cases get resolved in favor of the person suing, not me, which put stomach into a permanent knot. I felt angry, frustrated, and sad, especially with my cheerleader Mom gone. Forever. Sad that I thought these women were friends and sad that people could be like that. I worried that it all would affect my relationship with Phyllis, especially after honoring my contract to the gig in Palm Springs the day after mom died, but more than anything else I was disappointed in myself. How could I not have seen any of it? If that woman with the big envelope hadn't been walking up my mother's sidewalk when she did, how long would it have taken me to find out my mother's caregivers were thieves? I had played racquetball with one of them and felt close to her. She had never been in jail or in trouble before and I kept saying to Sandra, "She doesn't know. She is blinded by her partner. She's not a sociopath. She's being duped too."

I was so sure of that I put a note on her car letting her know what her partner was doing. She shared it with her partner and it got added on to the "harassment" claims, putting my stomach in knots all over again. How could I have been so stupid and naive? How could I have been such a poor judge of character? I was sure she couldn't have been part of it, but she was.

Since the police were involved, I was afraid that the Santa Maria Times would get wind of a lesbians vs. lesbians drama.

On the day of the hearing we took off work, and Sandra drove us to Santa Barbara. Once in the courthouse we sat in a small room by ourselves, but we could see Mom's caregivers, and my stomach turned again. I had a big box of notebooks filled with all the information we could possibly need about them. Sandra and I sat in the quiet room for a long time alone until our lawyer, dressed in a dark suit joined us. What was he going to say? I couldn't read his face. Please tell us anything good. Anything good, I said in my head.

"I threatened to bring up their criminal history," he said in a deep voice, "as well as the one's jail-time, and their numerous previous lawsuits, and they dropped the case."

Sandra and I inhaled at the same time.

"Oh my God. Thank you, thank you, thank you," I said.

We couldn't celebrate too much because they were still in mom's house telling the police we were harassing them, but *this* frightening $60,000 lawsuit was over. The thought that they would drop the case at the very last second never entered our minds. We were so ecstatic when we left the building I said, "Sandra, let's find a really nice restaurant. We've earned it."

She smiled. "I'm ready!" It had been a long time since either of us had smiled. Mom would have been pleased.

Though they were still in Mom's house it was much less stressful than being sued for $60,000, but I kept imagining them purposely destroying Mom's house.

Eventually a neighbor of mom's called to tell me she was watching them move out. I thanked her with flowers. I worried about what the house would look like, but as we pulled into the driveway it felt so good, even knowing Mom wasn't there. I felt such a connection just sitting in her driveway. We got out of the car with apprehension, slowly walked to the front door, and looked inside before crossing the threshold. "Thank God they didn't destroy Mom's house. They even left it in decent condition. "Thank you, God. Thank you, Mom. I know you are up there. They didn't destroy your house."

Before everything happened, the one I thought was a best friend asked if I minded if she got a job, because mom didn't need much help; she just needed someone around. I called a supervisor at VTC and told her my mother had a care giver that was looking for a job and mom didn't need her during the day because the second care giver was there. "Are there any job openings at VTC?"

"Yes, there are," the supervisor told me. I went over to mom's and told my friend there was a job opening at VTC if she wanted to apply and I told her I put in a good word for her. She was grateful and got the job - until I found out they stole social security numbers. The second I found that out I called VTC. The supervisor assured me that the thief couldn't get access to that kind of information and that she and her staff would keep an eye on her and never leave her alone. They couldn't fire her because she was a good worker, and they didn't want a lawsuit similar to mine. I apologized for being such a poor judge of character, which was putting it mildly.

About a month later the supervisor called me and sure enough, my ex-friend was suing VTC. She had figured out a way to get some kind of wage because she was forced to leave the area, so she was entitled to some kind of compensation.

In another act of unbelievable hubris she claimed that she had to leave the area because Barbara Wilson was sexually harassing her. This was the friend I thought was being duped by her partner. Can you imagine if the Santa Maria Times had gotten hold of *that* story?

They didn't win the lawsuit, but can you imagine me having to show up as a witness to refute *those* charges?

I was on a fast track to become an older but wiser Barbara.

TEN

Retirement (Age 57 & 59)
Hosted a retirement party

Sandra and I were getting too many weekend jobs in Palm Springs and arriving home late on Sunday nights to crawl into bed and get up on Monday morning for work. We talked to the district, and they let her leave her job teaching third grade to team teach my class which was fun. Sandra's artistic abilities helped, and we had Audrey as an outstanding assistant. Sandra and I taught two half days and stayed all day Wednesday to get our lesson plans and paperwork done. Teaching half days turned out to be a perfect way to get ready for retirement.

After retiring together we hosted a retirement party at the Lompoc Elks for every student and staff member from my thirty-three years at Martha Negus. Families I hadn't seen for thirty years showed up. The therapy unit came and helped find people from years ago, and the students from our current class did a magic show for about 120 people. The Lompoc Elks Club helped too.

I showed a video entitled Through The Years, and Josh Walton had a great slideshow from his years at Martha Negus. It was cool seeing how my previous students had grown and great to be in touch with their families again. Sandra was hostess extraordinaire even though the Elks provided the food. I got great cards from everyone, and they talked about their years at Martha Negus which is what I asked for as a retirement gift. I held back tears all day. It was a perfect ending to a perfect career and particularly special for Sandra and I to experience together.

We later found out that the bonus the district gave that year was based on our half salaries. Thirty years with the district, and that one year was all that mattered which was a disappointment, but there was nothing we could do about it.

ELEVEN

Life on Celebrity Cruises
2005
(More in An Older And Wiser Somebody)

I dreamed about entertaining on a cruise ship, but true to form I never did anything to make it a reality. I had no clue how to go about doing that and was sure they didn't hire people who were over-weight and unattractive, but whenever anyone asked if I had ever been on a cruise I chuckled. "I'm waiting 'til they pay me," then it happened! A gentleman named Mike Harris at a gig at Leslie's house in Palm Springs said, "You're a perfect cruise band." He got us a job on Celebrity Cruises the same year we were retiring and didn't ask for anything in return, so we took him to dinner.

November 18, 2005

Our trip was a nightmare. We were supposed to be on the ship two days ago and didn't go to bed before we left Santa Maria at 3:00 a.m. because we wanted to be tired enough to sleep on the plane. Our flight got fogged in at the Santa Barbara airport causing us to miss our Miami connection. Santa Barbara rerouted us to Dallas where we had the worst travel experience of our lives. We ran carrying my guitar, trumpet, and two carry-ons to counters with destinations to anywhere in Europe, then we ran to a gate hoping to catch a flight to London, but there were no passengers even taking up one chair. Devastated, we set everything down and sat alone trying to catch our breath.

"I can't believe this," Sandra said. "We have to go all the way back to where we can buy a ticket and try to find any flight that will get us across the ocean."

We picked up my instruments and carry-ons and hurried back to the counters dodging most of the crowd headed for their gates. When we got back to the ticket counters, Sandra saw a flight to Germany so we ran for that gate but missed that flight. Out of breath with no passengers in the waiting room we were frustrated.

"I can't believe this! Back to the ticket counters," Sandra said as we picked up our luggage again.

We missed four possible flights, each time going through security trying to find a connection to Barcelona! Four times we ran to booking desks, went through security, stood in lines, took our shoes off and put them on again as fast as possible before running to gates where the planes had just left.

We gave up catching an international flight and I talked Sandra into flying to Miami, assuring her we would be able to get a flight from there to anywhere in the world any time of day or night because Miami is a hub airport. We found a ticket counter with a direct flight from Dallas to Miami and got to Miami at 9:00 pm., but Miami was empty! No staff and no passengers. It felt eerie and the total opposite of what I assumed. Now Sandra and I had to walk around the empty airport looking for a phone booth. We found one against a wall and it took us another half hour to locate a hotel room near the airport. We called a cab to drive us to a hotel which was over ten miles away which was the closest we could stay near the airport. We checked ourselves into a room and we laid our heads down at about 1 a.m. We had been awake for over forty hours without sleep, and we had no clue where our luggage was.

Even after being up for forty hours, it was hard to sleep when we couldn't reach anyone at Celebrity. We kept calling the one number we had, and no one answered. The Millenium was sailing for Barcelona to pick up passengers the following day and as tired as we were, we were scared to fall asleep and miss getting a flight out as soon as the Miami airport opened, and we still didn't have a flight yet. On top of that we still didn't know where our luggage was.

We finally got a flight to Madrid from Miami and arranged to fly in a small Cessna type airplane to a small coastal town in Northern Spain where the Millenium had been in dry dock. At that airport we spotted a VIP with "Celebrity Cruises" written across her bag and we latched on to her, wondering if they would have found and picked us up if it hadn't been for her.

Next came a long van ride with Sandra and I struggling to stay awake while everyone chatted with us, then there it was. Our ship.

Finally. We made it three hours before it was due to sail tired, excited, and relieved.

We were so late they had removed the gangway in preparation for the ship's departure. We heard our driver making arrangements for how to get us on board without a gangway. I couldn't understand what they were talking about, then we were instructed not to get out of the van. A gigantic crane swung in our direction and gently dropped a humongous open metal container in front of our van. Sandra and I and the VIP got out of the van and went into the container feeling like ants inside a box. They put our carry-ons and instruments in with us and lifted us onto the ship's helicopter pad with a crane which was exciting!

Our next shock was our tiny room which only had a bunk bed, but we were so exhausted we fell asleep together on the bottom bunk still feeling insecure and out of sync with our new time zone. We agreed that if someone knocked on our door, we weren't going to let anyone know we had arrived. We needed sleep badly.

We were sure that since we were so late someone else took our assigned room and believed we were in a crew room. The bathroom was like an airplane bathroom with a shower, and our floor was sticky, but we had room service everyday so we put our used towels on our floor and used them as rugs. We were spoiled by our steward who was from India. He got our singing outfits dry-cleaned free and we tipped him for taking such good care of us.

Sandra was in an "I don't ever want to do this again," mode. But I wasn't. I knew things had to get better and we would reap the benefits of all our planning and nightmare days and nights.

We attended several important meetings, but within the first week passengers and staff told us daily how much they loved our music. "Sisters?" some would ask. Most passengers thought Sandra and I were twins. "Just friends," we explained. We stayed in the closet and never told a soul we were a couple. No one asked, "Can you play any Holly Near?" and we never met another gay couple on the staff or as passengers.

We slept together on the bottom bunk bed and gave ourselves space in our tiny room by storing our music equipment and other odds and ends on the top bunk which created a "psssst" from the staff who cleaned our room to let their buddies know, "That's them." They might have just as well pointed at us.

Entertaining on a cruise ship started out as an A+++ gig. We heard daily," You guys are fabulous," from our fellow musicians, staff, and passengers which filled us with such joy, pride, and confidence. The entertainment director often pulled us aside and said, "The passengers love you guys. You're like a cult." He was also kind enough to share with us that the cruise director liked us too, then those cruise and entertainment directors got relocated and everything changed.

Originally our hours were from 7 to 11. Now we were required to play until midnight which wasn't so bad but after we finished our gig we had to sign a timecard upstairs on the opposite end of the ship which meant carrying my trumpet and Sandra carrying my guitar to a room that was more than fifteen minutes away, at midnight. My feet hurt, so I took my heels off and tried to balance them on my trumpet case, but they kept falling off. Sandra worried we would get caught walking in stocking feet so she kept her heels on. When we arrived at the office we had to wait in line with other a musicians, then our boss handed me a timecard, and I wrote that we left our lounge at 12:15.

"Did you leave the lounge at exactly 12:15?" he asked.

"Well, around then," I answered.

"I don't want 'around then.' I need to know *exactly* what time you left."

It was humiliating.

"This isn't worth it," Sandra decided.

I had to agree. "Yeah, not worth it"

At Christmas we had fulfilled our contract, so we let the new director know we were disembarking in Florida. It took a bit of planning for Sandra and I to figure out what to do with our clothes and instruments. Renting a car and getting to my sister, Phyllis's house at Lake Anna Virginia seemed easiest, then we could ship stuff home from there.

We spent Christmas with Phyllis's large family. The tree already had presents galore and Santa hadn't even been there yet. Sandra and I borrowed Phyllis's car to do last-minute Christmas shopping. Several of the kids baked cookies for Santa Claus to eat on Christmas Eve. I had forgotten how exciting it was to spend Christmas with kids who still believed in Santa Claus. Christmas morning was everything we could expect. We took turns opening presents so we could see all the cool stuff everyone got and Phyllis had turkey dinner and rutabagas and garlic black olives.

On December 28th Phyllis took Sandra and I to the airport and all we had was one suitcase each. Phyllis shipped everything else to us in Santa Maria. It was the first time in my adult life I didn't have a paying gig on New Years Eve. Sandra's boys were all in their twenties and we had a belated Christmas celebration with them and their significant others. Looking back I would love a cruise gig that would respect me as a musician, not a roadie. Sandra enjoyed the job too because we got to entertain, eat great food, and travel in addition to a generous paycheck.

I proposed to Sandra on our 20th Anniversary even though we weren't allowed to marry at that time which I thought was clever, but it wasn't. Sandra was much more into our Solheim Cup golf trip and forgot to tell me she found a golf ball in her bag when we weren't golfing together. When I asked her if she found a special ball in her bag, her logical take on it was, "Yes, but we already know we're going to be together forever so you don't need to propose."

She wrote "Yes" on the ball and we kept it as a reminder that we are indeed committed forever, so I wouldn't change a thing.

TWELVE

Delta Kappa Gamma
Honorary Teacher's Sorority

Sandra and I were invited to become members of Delta Kappa Gamma, an honorary teacher's sorority. You need to have a sponsor to become a member of DKG. Nancy Straight sponsored Sandra, and Lou Emmons sponsored me. It would have been embarrassing for one of us to be asked to join and not the other. DKG meets at member's homes and neither of us ever felt anything but acceptance and respect from every member. No one cared that we were gay and would have protected us rather than get us fired. We never sat next to each other at the meetings because we wanted to talk to other people. I was in charge of music each year and Sandra held several different positions. The dues we paid went to causes like "Books for Babies" and college scholarships.

There were formalities for being sworn in, and I couldn't resist trying to amuse the teacher interviewing me with a quiet and sarcastic, "And I left the Catholic Church for this?" It was a formal swearing-in with candles, repeating promises, and singing the Delta Kappa Gamma song, and it is a worthy, interesting, and fun group, but Sandra and I quit when we tired of driving a half hour to Lompoc from Santa Maria every month.

Sandra has reminded me since that they wanted her to be President, and she would have liked to do that, but I didn't want to commit to the commute to Lompoc from Santa Maria. I still don't want to commit to the commute.

We had the pleasure of being Bailey's babysitter every summer for several years. She was sweet, enthusiastic, and loving. Mom lived with us after she had her stroke and she and Bailey bonded, but mom pointed out that I was taking a lot more photos of Bailey than of her. Sandra and I never showed affection in front of her boys but I made it a point to hold hands while watching TV and to kiss Sandra 'Hello' and 'Goodbye' in front of Bailey so she could see how natural it was.

One day Jon asked Sandra to explain our relationship to Bailey and Sandra was happy to do it. While Bailey was visiting us Sandra told her that her dad wanted us to talk to her about something. Bailey sat quietly and looked at her Nana and Sandra started, "Bailey, there are different types of families. Some with a mother and a father. Some with one mom. Some with one dad, and some families have two moms or two dads. Families with two moms or two dads love each other just like the families with one mom and dad. Barbara and I are like a two mom family or two nanas in your case."

We gave Bailey a minute to let that sink in before Sandra asked, "Do you have any questions, Bailey?"

"Can I have some pancakes?"

Sandra and I burst out laughing. I think the conversation was important but kinda "Duh" for Bailey who already knew her nanas loved each other, and we were all her family

THIRTEEN

Iwanaka Reunion
Sandra at her finest

Sandra must have had a sense of 'It's Now or Never' because she organized an Iwanaka reunion in Vegas in early 2007 to please her mother. Her parents and her brother Wayne needed wheelchairs to get to Circus Circus. I was "Sandra's friend" at the reunion and sat at the welcoming table to give at least fifty relatives a packet Sandra had organized. I felt like my pride for her was written all over my face as each relative mentioned how appreciative they were of Sandra organizing the reunion. She had name tags in the packet for each family.

They wrote the names of each person in their family and tacked it on a giant bulletin board in its proper place. Marilyn and Joe's name sat at the top and within an hour everyone could see a giant family tree with Marilyn's name at the top. She saw family she hadn't seen in years and never stopped talking. Joe was in his glory too. Wayne's wife Carol came, knowing it would be the last time she would see him, and a relative from Germany who was close to Sandra attended to Sandra's great delight. Most of the families had never met their relatives, and the room buzzed with laughter and non-stop chatter.

When it came time for the family photos and the shuffling of babies to great grandparents trying to find a spot where everyone could be seen. I wasn't in the photos but was thrilled be the designated photographer. "Take it with this camera please" made me feel important.

The reunion defined Sandra and her thoughtfulness combined with her smarts and organizational skills. Being her "friend" gave me plenty of recognition.

Sandra's parents needed help and wanted Sandra and I to provide it, which we did, but only as a stop-gap measure while we looked for suitable care. We hired someone to care for them at their home during the day, but that lasted less than a week because Marilyn said she caught the caregiver and Joe making out in the garage.

Joe was about eighty. What could we do? We apologized to the poor woman and let her go, then found someone else to take care of them.

"She stole my jewelry," Marilyn said in distress. We looked all over the house for her jewelry box and couldn't find it anywhere. With no explanation of where it could be, we had to let that woman go, too.

Weeks later, Sandra found the jewelry box hidden in a cabinet under the TV. We didn't know whether it was hidden as a reason to fire the caregivers or hidden from possible thieves.

One Sunday Sandra and I took Joe and Marilyn to brunch in Santa Maria and stopped at Merrill Gardens, the nicest care facility in the area. We thought the professionals there could explain to Joe and Marilyn why their lives would be enriched by moving there. It had a dining room, card games, music, craft activities, field trips including the casino, and 24 hour care. Sandra and I listened hoping they might consider it an easier way of life, but they weren't. They never even got to the cost before Joe let us know that we were wasting our time. He was not going to leave his house. I don't know how Marilyn felt, but she was a moot point since Joe was so against it, and his motto was, "There can only be one captain of the ship."

A saint appeared when Sandra's brother Wayne retired as the editor of the Lompoc Record and relieved us of our care-giving duties. He gave a month's notice at his apartment, got rid of most of his furniture and belongings, and moved in with Joe and Marilyn. There were no words to express our indebtedness to him. Since there could only be one captain of the ship, we felt Wayne was taking on an impossible task. Their parents weren't that physically disabled; they were more emotionally and mentally dysfunctional and hard to be around, and Wayne was moving in with them full time. We called him Saint Wayne when their parents weren't within ear shot.

Since Wayne was taking care of their parents, Sandra and I signed up for a two week trip to Africa with a group of gay men and women from Palm Springs. It sounded like an easy way to travel but it wasn't.

We missed all the meetings and were supposed to catch up by reading the material, calling people, and getting shots before it was scheduled to depart from Palm Springs, five hours away. I realized that it was much easier for Sandra and I to travel by ourselves than join someone else's planned trip.

While preparing for this trip of a lifetime, Wayne was diagnosed with colon cancer. He had just retired, but instead of enjoying it he moved in with his unreasonable parents. He always joked that, "the two worst things in this life are the holocaust and colonoscopies." If he had gotten a colonoscopy two years earlier when his doctor recommended it, it probably would have saved his life. Now he had painful colon cancer and needed chemo treatment and a lot of care. We were heartbroken and invited him to move in with us. He was grateful, and we helped him move in with us which meant their difficult needy parents would be living alone again.

We told Wayne we would cancel our trip to Africa because we had cancellation insurance, but when we called the insurance company they told us we only qualified for our money back if we had a letter from our doctor stating we were too ill to travel. Having a brother we were the caregiver for didn't qualify!

Sandra and I couldn't leave Wayne, even if it meant losing a lot of money. We told him we were cancelling the trip and he weakly breathed out, "Don't do that, I'll call Carol," his ex-wife.

Carol said she was happy to come help take care of Wayne and Joe and Marilyn for the two weeks Sandra and I would be in Africa. We picked her up at the airport and couldn't stop hugging her. We had two Saints in the family now, Saint Wayne and Saint Carol.

Sandra and I packed our new camera bag and telephoto lens and other stuff we were instructed to bring into the back of our Prius and made the five hour trip Palm Springs the day before we were to meet our group and fly to Africa. We are usually silent as we travel, but this time we were distraught about Wayne and even more distraught about leaving him.

"There's no way we can enjoy a trip to Africa while Wayne is dying at home in our bed," I said to Sandra. "Forget about the cancellation money. We can't go. We will be thinking about Wayne the entire time."

"I know," Sandra said. "How is Carol going to take care of Wayne and Mom and Dad?"

We determined that there was no way we could enjoy a trip to anywhere knowing that Wayne was dying, so we decided to lose the cost of the trip and get back to Wayne and Carol as soon as we could.

Sandra called the organizer from the car while we continued the five-hour drive in a fog. He reminded us we would lose the price of the trip and we told him we thought it was a horrible and heartless policy, but we understood."

We pulled into our already booked hotel, found our room and crashed on the bed without eating or changing into pajamas, physically and emotionally exhausted. During the night I awoke to hear Sandra throwing up.

"You know what?" She said. "I'm so stressed it's made me sick. Honestly. I'm a wreck." In spite of exhaustion she stayed awake most of the night. When we got up early the next morning we called a Palm Springs doctor and made an appointment." Sandra had a fever and chills and what appeared to be flu. The doctor confirmed her illness and I drove home the next day while Sandra slept.

We were still exhausted and Sandra couldn't see Wayne for fear of spreading her flu to him, but at least we were home in our own bed near him. When we finally got some sleep and felt good enough to get dressed we went to Wayne's room. We didn't think it was possible for him to be skinnier but he was.

"You shouldn't have canceled your trip," he said with weak breaths. We explained that Sandra got sick and his sickly lips smiled. We obviously made the right decision. The next day we took Carol to the airport and none of us could stop crying as we bid her goodbye. We hugged for what felt like forever with each of us crying as much as the next person.

FOURTEEN

An Unbelievable Act
Life Changer For Everyone

One night at around midnight, as difficult as it was for Wayne to get out of bed, he hobbled to our side of the house and knocked on our bedroom door. Did he need a ride to the hospital? We opened our bedroom door to see Wayne weak and spent.

"Mom called me. Dad just shot himself."

There is no way to describe the overwhelming emotions that hit us all at once. We stood in the doorway silent and stunned. "That's all Mom said," Wayne continued.

Sandra and I helped him back to his room. "We'll keep you informed" Sandra assured him.

We got out of our pajamas, grabbed coats, slammed the front door, and ran to the car. I hastily backed out of the driveway and sped on an empty highway toward their house in Lompoc. The usual twenty-five minutes was cut in half. Had the police been around they would have surely stopped me.

On the way I said to Sandra, "It looks like Joe made good on his promise to never leave his home and his knife and gun collections." I paused wondering if I should say my next thought aloud. "I shouldn't say it, but I believe life is going to be a whole lot easier for Marilyn now."

As we turned onto Pine Street we saw flashing lights from six police cars. All I could think of was the neighbors being disturbed in the middle of the night by those flashing lights shining in their windows. Couldn't they turn them off? Why were they still flashing?

Next we saw the yellow police tape stretched across the front yard keeping people out. What people? It was past midnight. The police were everywhere but the driveway wasn't blocked so I parked there. We jumped out and were surrounded by the police who accompanied us into the house where more policemen waited. "This is my parent's house," Sandra informed them.

We saw Marilyn talking rapidly to one of the policemen and she relaxed a little when she saw us. Sandra stood in front of the policeman and put her arm around Marilyn and discovered blood all over Marilyn's clothes, so she was a suspect. The police and Marilyn took us to the bedroom where a policeman informed us that had called 911. No one knew how she got blood on herself, and the walls and carpet in the bedroom were wet with blood splattered all over. Gruesome would be putting it mildly.

My legs went weak and I went to the living room to sit down and put my head in my hands, trying not to faint. Thankfully, Joe's body wasn't there for us to see. We never figured out how Marilyn got blood on her and whether she was in the room when he shot himself. It wasn't a question anyone but a policeman should ask. The room was so bloody it made sense that some of the blood ended up on her clothes.

Sandra and I assumed Joe was dead. She came and sat beside me on the couch, pale. "Dad's alive. The policeman said he's at a hospital in Santa Barbara. He had a concussion when his head hit the wall and a hematoma from the gun wound."

"He shot himself in the head and survived?" This was horrifically bad news. Sandra stayed beside me. We were weak and shaking, trying not to throw up. Marilyn was still talking 100 miles an hour to the policemen. They had to cut a big hole in the bedroom wall to get the bullet.

Sandra walked on shaking legs back to the bloody bedroom to get clothes for her mother and helped her change her bloody clothes in the bathroom while Marilyn continued talking 100 miles an hour.

"We need that for evidence," a policeman said to Sandra who handed Marilyn's bloody gown to them too shocked and overwhelmed to ask if her mother was a suspect.

It took forever for the police to leave, but we were finally able to lock the house and drive Marilyn home with us. She still couldn't stop talking. I wished I could understand her, but she talked so fast it was like listening to someone speaking a foreign language.

When we pulled into our driveway, Wayne got up to see Marilyn, even though it was 4:00 in the morning and he was weak. We sat in the living room while Marilyn continued speaking furiously. I couldn't understand a word she was saying, but Wayne and Sandra asked her questions and understood the conversation. Sandra gave her a glass of water and helped her to bed in our second guest room a couple of hours later.

Sandra and I visited Joe the next day in Santa Barbara while Wayne and Marilyn rested at our house. They admitted Joe to Santa Barbara instead of Lompoc because he was a suicide risk. The hospital was easy to find, but when we opened the door to his room I was flooded with emotion. It was like visiting a corpse with a bandage around its head.

He refused to move to a nice care facility for this? Everyone was angry with him and Marilyn didn't want to see him. When he had a stroke we drove her that same distance every day to visit him, but not this time. It was such a violent selfish act, that no one could forgive him. The captain of the ship chose bloody violence over a better life in an assisted living facility? If he could no longer face life, pills would have been traumatic, but a better choice than violence. When I suggested we go see a counselor, I wasn't taken seriously.

Marilyn lived with us now and saw how ill Wayne was becoming. Sandra and I taught and were busy with music gigs and taking care of Wayne. He helped us prove to Marilyn how much better off she and everyone else would be if she was living in an assisted living facility instead of watching Wayne painfully die and fortunately, she didn't resist.

After moving into the care home we picked Marilyn up every week and took her to the casino in Santa Ynez. She had an amazingly good disposition considering all that was happening in her life and was grateful for our attention and seemed happy in the facility. Joe was improving in Santa Barbara but was still in the hospital and it was hard for us to respect him and his selfish actions.

While dealing with Joe, the bloody house, and Joe's doctors, Wayne got worse at our house. He didn't want hospice to come to the house, but he ended up in so much pain we decided he would be more comfortable in the hospital where they could monitor his pain. Wayne was in so much pain before he died, we couldn't even drive him to the hospital. Marilyn was with us when the ambulance came to take her son to the hospital to die. You could see the sadness on her face, but she didn't want to see him carried out of our house to the ambulance. Sandra and I drove her back to her care facility, and we stayed in the hospital and never left Wayne's side for two days as he slowly, sadly passed away two weeks after Joe shot himself.

FIFTEEN

Russel Wayne Stockton
Saint Wayne

Wayne's celebration of life was at the Lompoc Elks Club. As is so often the case we found out much more about him after he died. He was quite an influence in the TV News industry. His death, photo, and accomplishments were broadcast on KVUE in Austin, Texas where he had been a news director for eleven years. His forte had been taking struggling stations and bringing them into number one spots. We found out how respected and loved he was when so many people from Texas spoke at his memorial. His job in Lompoc was editor of the Lompoc Record until he felt an obligation to help his parents. Sandra's sons all spoke at the memorial.

Wayne was truly a Saint.

Marilyn was at the service devastated to lose her beloved son. Joe couldn't make it as he was bedridden. We never told him that Wayne died, because we felt it would have added to his confused state. Wayne had been close to his mom but not to his dad. His moving to their house was for Marilyn's benefit, not Joe's. Each time we saw Joe he inevitably said something critical about Wayne.

Sandra Marilyn and I were still upset with Joe for shooting himself and it was hard to visit him, particularly when he was now an hour away in Santa Barbara. When he had a stroke we drove Marilyn to Santa Barbara every day to visit him, but not this time.

The police ended up with Joe's weapons because Sandra and I didn't want to deal with them. Joe loved them, but it was a relief for Sandra and I to be rid of them. The police could have them all.

When Joe began to improve he could talk and begged us to take him home. No answer would satisfy him, and there was no way in the world it was ever going to happen. It was sad and depressing, and we couldn't even get him into a nursing facility in Santa Maria because he was a suicide risk.

Marilyn became ill and was moved from the care home into a place that was like an extended hospital. Joe was in another wing of the same facility and we decided not to tell him she was there as we didn't know if seeing him would create more stress for her.

It was a hard call.

SIXTEEN

Tracey (Miller) Baker's Wedding And...
From Happy to Sad

Feeling a little sense of normalcy, we had to leave Sandra's parents to entertain for my Goddaughter's wedding in the upper peninsula of Michigan. Knowing Marilyn was ill made leaving her agonizing, but we had a long time commitment to the Miller family. We hadn't seen Sally and Bob for over twenty years, and this would be our first time meeting Tracey and her brother Bobby. Sally was my best friend from Jones Hall and was family to me and my parents.

We arrived two days before the wedding and stayed at their gorgeous home, a spitting distance from Monroe Lake and its fluorescent sky. We were greeted by hugs and laughter which brought the many years of Sally and Bob playing games at mom and dad's house to the forefront of our memories. It was great reconnecting and meeting their grown family. Eventually the conversation about me being gay came up and how I was responsible for the three women being expelled from Eastern Michigan University because of my homophobia. I could have this conversation with Sally because I had run to Sally's apartment for advice. I thought she was the one who told me to report Jane, but Sally said that wasn't true, and she was right. In my diary I saw that she thought the head advisor was being too harsh on Jane. I disagreed with Sally back then and didn't think being kicked out of college was too harsh a punishment for being a homosexual. According to my diary Sally wasn't home when I ran to her apartment, her roommates were. If Sally had been home, things may have turned out differently, but I had my mind made up to report Jane.

"You know Diane is gay," Sally said.

"You have got to be kidding!" In my memory I thought Diane was the head advisor when I reported Jane, but it was Mrs. Overgard who had followed her that I reported Jane to. I had driven Diane to the airport the year before when she left there. I liked and respected her so much I wondered if things would have been handled differently if she had been my head advisor, but it would have been an uncomfortable and unprecedented situation for a gay head advisor, especially since I was so freaked. I'm sure she would have been fired back then too. I don't know how Sally knew about Diane, but Diane wouldn't have invited me to her room with two women hugging on her bed.

Talking to Sally was like old times. I could hear many a cuckoo from a distant cuckoo clock when we talked late into the night even though we had to get ready for Tracey's wedding. We spent the next day choosing music and planning what music others would sing while Monroe Lake changed colors all day and became one of the most beautiful sunsets I had ever witnessed. I snapped my camera for an hour as the sunset changed from colorful to more colorful by the minute; Sally and her family got to see this every day. If you have to endure Michigan weather, they found a perfect spot to make the most of it.

At the wedding was perfection. Bob sang Heatland's "I Loved Her First" to Tracey impressing everybody with a powerful tear jerker. The wedding was flawless, then right after it we got the dreaded call that Marilyn had died.

"Oh no, not without us there." We sobbed, unable to catch our breath, regretful that we weren't there. We caught a flight and arrived home in a broken-hearted fog.

We had a memorial for Marilyn at the home where she lived. Many staff and residents attended as well as Sandra's family who all spoke fondly of Marilyn. She and I had grown to love and respect one another which seems miraculous after she had disowned us for so many years. She ended up introducing me as family and I would glow, but the irony was I was more uncomfortable about being outed as Sandra's family than she was. Once she accepted me as family there was no hiding it.

Good for Marilyn.

SEVENTEEN

Scam or Unbelievable Coincidence
Which one is it?

Nine months after Marilyn passed we got a call that Joe was dying. He had lived for a couple of years in different hospitals and homes after his suicide attempt. I went to the home he was in and got to be with him when he took his final breath which made me feel closer to him. Sandra arrived shortly after. It surprised me how sad and painful his passing was and how much I regretted not visiting him more and for not being more forgiving. He had gone from disowning us to being able to tell me I was the best thing that ever happened to Sandra, but I hadn't been as generous with my forgiveness toward him after he shot himself.

Joe didn't have any friends at that point in his life, so we had a small memorial at our house with family. Sandra lost both parents and her brother in that same nine month period, and our grief and stress felt never ending. Sandra was strong through it all as she planned one memorial after another.

Two days after Joe died, Sandra received an email that stated, "I have your dad's military dog tags."

Sandra and I learned to recognize a scam when we saw it, and this looked like the ultimate scam. I am the trusting one, and I said to Sandra, "What an unconscionable thing to do; call every person who has placed an obituary and tell them you have that person's dog tags. How creepy is that? Maybe he makes them. Who would fall for that?"

Sandra got a call from a relative who told her, "Someone is trying to contact you."

It's a scam," Sandra said.

"He said New Jersey," her cousin added.

"It's a scam," Sandra repeated - "Wait! Did you say New Jersey?"

"Glassbourgh, New Jersey."

Sandra fell silent for awhile, then said, "Mom and Dad lived there."

"Well, a guy found Joe's dog tags and I don't think it's a scam," her cousin said. "He's interested in talking with you. I think you should answer his email."

Here are the emails about Joe's dog tags.

Hey Sandra,

Just to confirm I have the right "Joe Stockton" here's what's stamped on the tag

Joseph R Stockton

697-8509 T 42 T44 O

Marilyn Stockton

Box 194

Honolulu. Hawaii. TH F

I currently live in Tallahassee, Florida, but I am a native of Pittman New Jersey and my grandmother lives in Glassboro, New Jersey, the next town over. Several years ago she had a new driveway cut and graded which then was covered with stones. My wife and 20-month-old twin sons visited with her in July of this year and took them on a walk. As we were walking out of the driveway, the sun caught something that glimmered. Turned out to be a shard of broken glass and looking around, it turns out that there was quite a bit of broken glass mixed in with the gravel. Since the driveway isn't terribly large, I attempted to pick up all the pieces (at least all of the larger problematic pieces anyway) And oddly enough, Joe Stockton 's dog tag was in my grandmother's driveway.

My grandfather passed in January of this year but had served with the navy during World War II in the South Pacific. I briefly entertained the possibility that my grandfather found the tag in the 40s and brought it back with them, but my grandmother said she's never heard of Joe, nor has any idea why his tag would be in her driveway. My grandparents talked about everything so if it were indeed my grandfather who retrieved the tag my grandmother would've known about it.

So best I can tell, Joe's tag was debris included among the broken glass in with the stones delivered to my grandmothers driveway in Glassboro. Strange right?

Did Joe ever walk a dog near a quarry? I don't know anything more than what I related above.

Anyway, if I have the right person and you give me a mailing address I'll gladly send it along to you this week.

David Hutton

PS Another possibility is my grandparents used to own a lake house in Glassboro. In fact, my grandmother still lives at the house my grandfather built there in the 1950s. It's possible Joe came to the lake and lost his tag which was then un-earthed when the driveway was graded a couple years ago.(And later still)

Hey Sandra,

I just checked with my grandmother. My understanding of the timeline was a bit off. My grandparents bought Lake Oberst from Mrs. Oberst in 1955. Mrs. Oberst herself bought the lake around the early 1930s, and the cottage itself dates from the 1920s. The lake was open for business as long as Mrs. Oberst owned it and presumably even before then, up until my grandparents finally closed it in 1972.

So it's still possible your folks either lived at one of the cottages or lost the tag while walking in the woods during a visit to the lake.

Hey Sandra,

See the attached. I haven't attempted to clean or polish it or anything. The actual tag is more dull in appearance than my camera flash and Photoshop may have you believe.

You and I are separated by a generation. My parents are (illegible)Glassboro. It's my grandma's mom's dad who served in the Navy during World War II and passed earlier this year which was well received by us as a blessing as he's been on the losing end of a battle with Alzheimer's for the past 10 years or so. Thanks for. (Illegible) Rough to lose so many people close to you, especially in such a short stretch.

Do you know the address of your folks former Glassboro address?

Here's a map showing Lake Oberst general location.
(Illegible link to Lake Oberst)

I believe around the time you were born, my grandparents and my mother's older brother lived on the office at side of the lake in (Illegible). for their next and final house.

In the mid-50s my grandfather broke ground and built the lakefront home in which my grandmother still resides. There were several existing cottages along the lake which were available for rent.

I'll call my grandmother later today and inquire as to exactly when they purchased the property and what she knows of the history of the property prior to their ownership. Perhaps your folks lived at one of the college cottages or perhaps your dad lost his tag one day. (Illegible). Too bad I couldn't have found out six months prior or else your dad might have explained it himself.

Other than that, I'm fairly savvy at finding people on the web. Less than 10 minutes of googling for Joseph Stockton and Marilyn who stopped in Hawaii in WW2 brought me to your father's memorial site at which point I was only about 99.44% sure I have the right family which is about as certain as I ever am of anything.

Don't sweat it. I understand your skepticism as there is a whole Internet full of weirdos out there. I suspected as much.

Sandra called Mr. Hutton and thanked him after apologizing for not believing him. He understood her skepticism, especially since it was only two days after Joe died. Sandra sent him a "Thank you" and a photo of the frame she put the dog tag in.

EIGHTEEN

Prop 8
November 2008 CA voters ban same gender marriage AGAIN!

Prop 8 came along in November 2008. Instead of Prop 22 supporters having regrets and learning from the suicides and destroyed families created by Prop 22, they dug their heels in to win at any cost. Believe you are a welcomed fanatic in Jesus's name? Pick Bible verses that support your lifestyle. So what if it causes depression and suicides and families being torn apart? It's a small price to pay to prevent same gender couples like Sandra and I from getting married.

$83 million dollars was raised to support or fight Prop 8 which was the same as Prop 22. Twenty million dollars was raised by the Church of Latter Day Saints. Over $3 million was raised by the Catholic Church and other religious sects. Even individuals gave up part of their earnings to make sure folks like us and tens of thousands of other gay couples who had been together for thirty forty and even fifty years couldn't get married. Can anyone think of a better way to spend that amount of money? $83 million dollars for signs and TV ads while people on the planet were starving and in physical pain.

I feel much better when I remind myself that if there is a judgement day…it will come for those people too.

How many wars are justified by religion? They are even called 'Holy' wars. Hitler's advisor's used Roman's 13 to recruit followers to believe in one pure race. What happened to "Love Thy Neighbor?"

There are 1000's of people throughout history who have been jailed because they believed they were acting on behalf of their God. You want to justify hating Jews? It's in the Bible. You want to justify hating blacks? It's in the Bible. You want to justify hating Muslims? It's in the Bible. You want to believe that only Christians are going to Heaven? It's in the Bible. You want to hate transgenders? It's in the Bible.

It's hate and a feeling of superiority, self-righteousness, and a justified opinion that the God who is on your side is cruel, deadly, and the opposite of what the Ten Commandments stand for.

NINETEEN

More Biblical "take it or leave it."

Deformed people cannot approach God. Leviticus 21-18-2

Non-virgins are to be stoned with rocks. - Deuteronomy 22:20-21

A Woman's punishment for defending her husband? - Cut off her hand. Deuteronomy 25:11-12

Giving birth to a daughter makes you unclean for 66 days - Leviticus 12-5

If you disobey God you will eat your babies Leviticus 26:27-30

If your brother dies and has no children you need to "raise up seed unto his brother." Mark 12-19

Cursing at your parents warrants death. Leviticus 20-9

Men with missing or wounded male parts are not allowed in church. Deuteronomy 21-1

Your family is your enemy, and you are all competing for God's love. Mathew 10-25-27

If you steal something or sin in any way, cut off your hand. Mark 9-43

Women will never teach or have authority over men. Timothy 2-11

Give a thief your belongings. Mathew 5-40

Invite your attacker to beat you more. Mathew 5-39

Even a look counts as adultery. Mathew 5-28

Anyone who curses in the name of Lord will be stoned to death. Leviticus 24:16

Anyone who works on the Sabbath is to be put to death. Exodus 31:15

Women must cover their hair during prayer -Corinthians 11-5

As if God cares what people wear when they pray. We have wonderful photos of us in our hats. If we visited a Church and didn't have our hats, mom would find Kleenexes to throw on our heads.

Incensed about Prop 8, I wrote this letter to our neighbors.

Dear Neighbors,

I can't express the confusion, hurt, and fear we feel as we drive down our street and see sign after sign of "Vote No on 8." I doubt any of you put up your sign with malice, but it would have been much kinder of you to just privately cast your vote in a voting booth.

I find it very interesting that drug addicts, alcoholics, thieves, verbal and physical abusers, child molesters, adulterers and some really bad people can all get married over and over again and still receive the legal benefits of marriage. Most surprising is that people feel SO STRONGLY about two people who love each other and who are committed to each other getting married. That's what marriage is about. Love and commitment.

I feel compelled in the midst of all the "yeses" to present our solo "no."

I hope that we can remain friends and continue to be supportive of one another, and I thank you for being the wonderful neighbors you have been over the years.

PS. I have no fear of God's judgement of me. It's people's judgement of me that is scary.

The good news was the two neighbors I spoke to about their 'No on prop 22 'signs didn't put out a "No on 8" sign and on June 26, 2013 the Supreme Court ruled that Proposition 8 was unconstitutional and same gender marriages joyously resumed.

TWENTY

Important Events
Pride Folks and Pride

Sandra and I were invited to two different condo vacations in Hawaii. Nancy and Sue who I met through my dental hygienist invited us to stay for a week at their time share and our neighbors Marney and MJ coordinated with them for all of us to be in Kauai at the same time.

The six of us snorkeled, hiked, listened to live Hawaiian music and ate the Hawaiian foods Sandra recommended. As soon as returned from staying with Marney, MJ, Nancy, and Sue in Hawaii, I flew alone to Virginia for Alyssa's wedding while Sandra packed our bags for an Alaska cruise with Anne, Ashley, Marney, and MJ and their best friend Patricia.

2016 (Age 68)
I got my hair done in a town a half an hour from Palm Springs and told the hair dresser I was going to Palm Springs the next day. She told me to be careful because there would be a lot of gays there that weekend. I'm ashamed that I made no comment, but as a stranger getting my hair done, I don't think I was going to change her perception of gays, but I can hope she doesn't have a daughter, granddaughter, or relative that hears her make such bigoted comments. Maybe someday she will be an older and wiser somebody.

2017 (Age 69)
Santa Maria hosted its first successful "Pride" event with a lot of help from my ex Clara's wife, Eva Didion. She and her committee

recruited local vendors, entertainment, and speakers and provided valuable information to people in a fun atmosphere for all. Hundreds of elated people of every age and nationality attended. In many ways that event started in the seventies at Lianne Hutton and Vivian Engel's house. Now there are so many events and organizations for lesbians that we have outgrown our women's raps. We still have movie nights, Emmy parties, football parties, or card-playing gatherings, and at least one lesbian book club, but we have outgrown the need to read books written only by lesbian authors. We haven't outgrown the need to be around other lesbians because it still feels good to know that every person in that room celebrates you and you can hold hands or snuggle next to your partner and be totally relaxed.

February 12, 2019

A teacher was fired because she married her beautiful lesbian partner and the video of the wedding was on Facebook. Three teachers were disciplined for attending the wedding. At least one parent who supported the teacher was upset at the Catholic school's decision.

Fifty years ago I didn't know any better when I destroyed the lives of three coeds and their families. Today there is no excuse for people still destroying families by being self-righteous and playing God which is further proof of why I had to be so closeted and scared when I taught.

TWENTY ONE

New Years Eve in Apache Junction AZ
P.I.C.K.L.E BALL! Pickleball!

One of the best things about our New Year's Eve gigs at the Pueblo or Superstition Mountain in Apache Junction Arizona is that we played pickleball or golf every day from December 27th through to December 31st.

When we start our gig at 9:00 the floor fills up with dancers. We stop the music around 11:00, and ask all the couples to grab their loved ones, and come out on the dance floor. After all the couples are on the floor I start singing "Through the Years," then "I Swear," followed by "Endless Love," and last, their favorite, "Could I Have This Dance."

With the dance floor packed I announced, "OK if you haven't celebrated your 20th anniversary yet please step aside." Hardly anyone steps aside. "25 years!" A few couples stopped dancing and joined the outer ring. Keeping the music going, I announced, "30 years!" and more couples are leaving the dance floor and joining the ring around the remaining dancers. "35 years!" The couples who have stopped dancing start whooping and hollering and praising couples together for 35 years. "40 years!" Two couples get an ovation as they leave the floor. "45 years!" The whoops and hollering grows intense as we get to "50, 51, 52, 53, 54,55,56,57,58... By 59 two couples are still on the dance floor and the noise from the room is deafening

"Sixty!"

"We celebrated our 60th they yell. Keep going."

"Us too," the one other couple yells as the crowd goes crazy. 61, 62. One couple exits to hugs and screaming.

"Keep going" the last elderly couple on the floor yell as they keep dancing.

63, 64, 65.

"65!" they yell. "65 years!"

The energy of this couple set the example for committed relationships is electric and indescribable. The most committed couples on the planet and they were still not allowed to marry? Sandra and I have done the same thing at straight country club parties and straight 55+ communities and there is no comparison to the love of the Apache Junction parties.

We ended the night close to 1 a.m. and someone invariably mentioned that we were the only group that kept the seniors up to an hour past midnight.

One year someone let us know that the special couple who had celebrated 65 years together died a day apart.

The day after the party Sandra and I played more pickleball to, "You guys were great. We had a blast," then we attended several New Years Day parties.

We headed home on January 3rd, stopping in Palm Springs for more Pickleball with friends. On the way home from Palm Springs I called the Santa Maria Rec Department from the car. "Do you have pickleball?"

"Do we have what?" The man acted like he misheard.

"Pickleball." I said again. "Do you have pickleball?"

"Pickleball?" He repeated sounding confused.

"Yes, pickleball. P I C K L E ball. Pickleball!"

This happened every year when we got back from our gigs at the Pueblo or Superstition Mountain.

I became addicted to pickleball there and on trips to Palm Springs, and come home and call the Santa Maria Rec department.

"Pickleball. P I C K L E ball! Pickleball. You need to learn about it."

After four years of that I decided that if I was ever going to play pickleball in Santa Maria, I had to take the initiative.

TWENTY TWO

We Bought a House
Pickleball

2011 (Age 63)

Sandra and I talked about moving during the George Bush era when the housing market was in the toilet. Many lawns on our long street were neglected, and some of them were so uncared for they looked as if no one lived in them. Even though most of the homes were still nice, it became depressing driving past the neglected ones.

"Let's think about moving," I said, "especially since the housing market is down."

With that in mind while bicycling past some houses in a nicer area of town when I saw a house with a 'For Sale' sign with a beautiful door. Everything about it looked inviting and the area was flat and perfect for bicycling. I wrote the address down and bicycled up our long hill back home. "Hey Sandra, I just saw a beautiful house with a beautiful door that I'd love for you to see."

"Let's call Ellen and see if she can show it to us tomorrow."

Ellen our realtor made arrangements to meet her the following day. With the address in hand I pulled up to the house with the gorgeous door and Ellen parked behind us. When we hopped out of our cars Ellen told us, "This is Jane Russell's house."

"What? You've got to be kidding! No way, Ellen! No way!"

"Yes, it is, honest."

Ellen opened the inviting front door and we stepped into a lovely entryway that led to a beautiful atrium.

"Oh my God, this is a gorgeous home. "Look at that!" I pointed. "There are still sayings and artwork on the wall and some of it is signed by Jane Russell. Proof that it's her house."

We could not believe this was happening. "We can invite Pat Brenner and all our friends from Palm Springs to stay with us in Jane Russell's house," I boasted.

Sandra grinned. "There is a master bedroom downstairs and upstairs. How perfect is that?"

The small backyard had grass along the back of the house.

"Easy to care for," Sandra said.

A sliding glass door led to the patio, a family room, and a master bedroom.

"Look at the atrium, Sandra. It's huge! Look at that ceiling. It's all glass that I bet will get dirty and need cleaning often."

"Yep," Sandra agreed. "It will require a lot of up-keep and outside help."

"It's gorgeous, though. I wonder if we can afford it? I'll bet it's overpriced because it's Jane Russell's estate," I whispered to Sandra.

We walked to the kitchen. "Okay Ellen, how much?"

She was ready for my question and quoted a fair price for the house.

"Oh my God, Sandra, we can afford this house," I squealed in front of Ellen, "And it's fairly priced."

"Okay, Ellen. We want to see it tomorrow, but we are ninety nine percent sure we want to buy it. Same time tomorrow?"

She nodded. "Sounds good."

The next day Ellen couldn't keep up with us as we practically ran to that exquisite front door and we couldn't believe we were the only people interested in Jane Russell's house which had just come on the market. This time we looked at the house through our eyes, and not through Jane Russell's.

"The walls are a little too froufrou for us," I laughed to Sandra.

"Yeah, they can be painted."

Once again, we were giggling and grabbing each other's hands, imagining calling our Palm Springs friends and asking if they would like to spend a weekend or week with us in Jane Russell's house. We couldn't believe our good fortune.

"That atrium is beautiful, but it's going to take a lot of care and upkeep," I said.

Sandra looked at me. "Yes, but it's worth it."

"Okay, Ellen, It' s a no brainer. We are going to buy it." Sandra and I held hands for a fraction of a second. This was all happening so fast it was beyond belief. We were buying Jane Russell's house, all because I bicycled past a door I fell in love with.

I took one more look at that attractive door when we headed back to our cars. That door is going to be ours, I thought. I pulled away from the house driving aimlessly and talking nonstop, heading to Ellen's office to sign the mounds of paperwork we knew awaited us.

Two minutes into our aimless drive to Ellen's office we passed another 'For Sale' sign next to our favorite house in all of Santa Maria.

"Why not just take a look at it?" I said to Sandra. I pulled over and Ellen pulled up behind us.

We walked into that house and saw it had a rustic fireplace and a rustic kitchen.

"Love it." Sandra and I looked at each other and went to a spacious four car garage lined with wall-to-wall shelving.

"Love it." We smiled at each other again and looked at the driveway.

"Oh my God, Sandra, this driveway is big enough for a pickleball court. Can you imagine? I could play pickleball every day?"

I asked the owner for a measuring tape while Sandra googled pickleball court dimensions. We stretched his measuring tape and sure enough, the driveway was big enough for a pickleball court. When we handed the measuring tape back to the owner, he said, "You would love the gals next door."

"The gals next door? In our favorite house?"

"One is a teacher and the other is a paralegal. I take care of their house, and they take me to dinner when they come to town."

A rustic home with room for ping pong table and a pickleball court next to our favorite house in Santa Maria which is owned by gals, plus storage throughout the house.

"Ellen, I can't believe we aren't going to buy Jane Russell's house, but someone else will love getting it. We feel more at home here and I can play pickleball every day."

That's how we ended up in a perfect house for us with Marney and MJ as neighbors.

Once we moved in we discovered Anne and Ashley three doors down from us and they had never met Marney and MJ, so the six of us hung out together as best friends. Even though Sandra preferred golf to pickleball and has a shoulder that gets aggravated with pickleball, it didn't stop her from figuring out everything we had to know about having our own pickleball court. We paved the driveway and our son Jason and grandson Braeden painted the court as my Christmas present — it was perfect.

The next order of business was finding someone to play with which was not easy. No one had heard of pickleball, and it's not something you can advertise in a newspaper. I called Santa Maria's Department of Recreation and Parks and told them, "If anyone calls and asks you about pickleball, here's my phone number."

"If they ask us about what?"

"Pickleball. P.I.C.K.L.E ball... .Pickleball! Here's my phone number. Have them call me."

No one called and my beautiful court sat unused until I explained my dilemma to my dental hygienist Sherry, who said, "I think my mom would like to try it. What is it called again?"

"Pickleball, and if you think your mom has the courage to knock on a total stranger's door, I have an extra paddle for her to try, and I would love to introduce her to pickleball."

When Sharon Hill knocked on my door, we hit it off like gangbusters. Her tennis skills transferred to pickleball skills in one day and after that one meeting, she felt comfortable enough to say, "I have another friend I'd love for you to meet."

"Absolutely! Bring her next week."

That's when I met Nancy and Sue from Pismo Beach, and Nancy fell in love with pickleball too. After that I got a call from Jerry and Mary Lou Thomason from Santa Maria who had called the Rec department hoping there was pickleball in Santa Maria. The Rec department gave them my number, and they started playing pickleball on my court.

I won't spend time writing about the meetings we had with the Rec department trying to get courts and places to play, but I will mention that they finally offered pickleball as a class, and ten years later we have a pickleball committee and eight fabulous courts with over a hundred players with more joining every day.

My court gets used several times a week with my favorite players, Holly, Cuca, Elly, Elisa, Alissa, Mary Perry, and Shelley. We promised to social distance, get our vaccinations, wear masks, and avoid anyone not vaccinated, or do anything to put any of us at risk, because we all have issues that could kill us or a family member if we got Covid. For some of us it meant not seeing family, but we get to safely and fearlessly see each other and play pickleball with each other.

Laughing.

TWENTY THREE

Denied Golf Membership
Hurt

Sandra and I were denied a couple's monthly membership at our local golf course which was surprising because we had played with many friends in Palm Springs whose status as a couple was respected. When the person behind the desk looked us in the eyes and told us we didn't qualify as a couple, my mouth fell open and my stomach twisted into a knot. Sandra started to pay full price and golf anyway until I gasped, grabbed her arm and said, "Sandra, we are not giving our money to this club. We will play elsewhere." Confrontation made me nauseated. Who the heck were they to tell us we weren't a couple? I suspected that the man behind the counter had been married several times.

We left him, and we couldn't stop talking about it the entire way home.

"I'm writing them a letter." I said.

"It won't do any good."

"I can't believe this. My mother wouldn't believe this. Who are they to tell us we aren't a couple? We're not a couple? Wait until we tell our friends in Palm Springs!"

"Let's call them when we get home. They won't believe it."

"I'm writing a letter." I said again.

"It won't do any good Hon."

"I think it's just the guy at the front desk. They can't *all* feel that way can they?"

I wrote them a letter as soon as we got home and I expected that someone would read the letter and override the actions of the person at the front desk. We waited for a call, a letter, an apology, or "We'd be happy for your membership," but it never came.

Sandra and I golfed elsewhere for about six months until the honorable Barbara Beck showed up at our house with a newspaper article that said two women sued their golf course and won the case, and that our course would have to accept our couple status. Sandra and I had a long discussion about whether we really wanted to play there knowing how they felt about us, but we had so many friends who respected us we didn't want to cut off our nose to spite our face, so we took the article and once again, with a knotted stomach told them they had to let us join as a couple.

The person we handed it to left the desk and handed it to someone in the office who said, "OK," and wrote up our couple's membership. My hands shook so badly I could hardly sign the paper.

Since then we have never felt uncomfortable with any staff members and we have always been treated with respect, but I sometimes wonder if they still don't recognize us as a couple.

We are so happy to golf every Thursday with some of the same women my mother golfed with. Sandra and I kept our couple status a secret from our lady friends for many, many years. If people noticed that Sandra paying for me, I'd say, "I buy Christmas presents for her kids, so it works out for her to pay for my golf."

As years have passed, there were golfers who let us know they weren't prejudiced and we could tell them, "Yes, we're a couple." Initially we asked for their secrecy, but after about ten years the word gradually spread throughout the club, and Sandra and I have never felt anything but acceptance and appreciation from every woman in the club.

TWENTY FOUR

What Is There Not To Love About Golf?
Lots

How about stupid rules? Some people claim there are no stupid rules but if there is a banana peel in the sand trap you can't move it! The book *Make The Hole Bigger* has humorous drawings that Sandra added and is filled with amusing takes on rules that seem to make game unfair, cause slow play, or other annoying golf rules and is available on Amazon and "Make The Hole Bigger.com" It makes a unique tee prize at a reduced price.

What do I regret about the book? I couldn't say, "The author has three bonus sons and six bonus grandchildren." because it would out us, and I wasn't going to say "Sandra has family and not say they are mine too, so I left everyone out.

Since Sandra and I are in Palm Springs the weekend of the LPGA for gigs, I wondered what a booth at the WLPGA would cost us to sell our book, and I wanted to advertise that 'Sound on Sound" entertains at golf events. The tournament is held at the Mission Hills Country Club in Rancho Mirage. Since Sandra has our TV tuned to the golf channel every day, I didn't think it would be hard to talk her into having a booth there, and it wasn't.

As it turned out we weren't allowed to sell anything, we could only promote it. By the time we found that out, Sandra was in heaven imagining spending four days at her favorite golf event. We were allowed to have three people man our booth. Our friend Helen Lovera was more than happy to spend the weekend with us, and icing on the cake was Jane Roscoe and Diane Gill who invited Helen to spend the weekend at their house.

The first morning of the tournament we were allowed to park our car next to our booth and load everything into it and manning the booth was fun. The professional golfers had to walk by our booth to get to the next hole and Sandra and Helen could leave the booth anytime to watch the tournament while I preferred talking to people and manning the booth as opposed to watching golf.

Sandra and I stayed with our friend Dorothy Reed and as a bonus we entertained at Dorothy's on Sunday and the "Never Too Old to Party" women's dinner dance Friday night at the Embassy Suites.

Financially the booth was a bust, but it was more fun than work. We gave a lot of books away and only got one job at the Mission Hills Country Club. As entertainers we used the same locker room as the professional golfers. We were in there by ourselves, so we examined their gold-plated names on the lockers and imagined them all in there together.

"Look Sandra, here's Nancy Lopez. Oh look, Michelle Wie. Here's Julie Davies. "Oh my gosh, Christina Kim."

We met a lot of interesting people from other booths and part of the fun was seeing friends from Palm Springs who were surprised to see our booth. The gig at the country club was for the Putting Club and it went OK, but I would have liked a mulligan to choose different songs.

TWENTY FIVE

Wilson/Thayer Challenge

Barbara is betting every team $5 that she and Noni can beat them. One person drives, the other one putts and anyone hits In between. Come join us for lunch at our home afterwards.

I created this challenge while golfing with Noni Thayer who was turning 90. It took her two drives to get to my one drive, but when we got to the green, she sank them while I three putted. Our final score was Thayer 101, Wilson 111.

I said, "Noni if we played as one person we could beat anybody."

Every year my long game ends up in the trees and sand and Noni puts them in for me. I have my favorite day of golf but we don't beat anyone because of my long game, so it costs me $5 bets that go to our club, and it's well worth it. One year when I was sick, Sandra and Noni played, and they beat everyone.

May 2021

The Rancho Maria women's golf team won the championship for the first time in 30 years and guess who was their enthusiastic captain and their competent enthusiastic co-captain?

Sandra Woo and Connie Phillips.

When I praise Sandra for this feat, she humbly reminds everyone that there are four new great players, and that's what made all the difference.

Planning the Wedding
June 28, 2017

Corinthians 13:4-8a

Love
Is patient and kind
Does not envy or boast
Is not proud or self-seeking
Keeps no record of wrongs
Is not easily angered
Does not delight in evil
But rejoices with the truth
Always protects, always trusts
Always hopes and perseveres
Love never fails

To my beautiful, loving, caring, honest, fun, easy-going, generous, adventurous, forgiving, witty, great cook, artistic, suma cum laude, listener with an easy smile who finds everything I lose and overlooks my many faults without complaint.

My lover for life.

Sandra wanted to wait until marriage was legal both federally and in the state of California when I decided I was ready to get married. All of Sandra's reactions were a good indication. It was me who wanted to get married when everything was legal.

Several years ago when we were passing The Cliffs in Pismo Beach, Sandra said, "If we ever get married, I'd like it to be at the Cliffs."

When I reminded her of this, she claimed she never said that, so if I misheard it, that means she never mentioned wanting to get married. Ever.

I have never doubted Sandra's commitment to me, but I wanted a wedding with our kids, grandkids, close friends to see us make our commitment. I went to the Cliffs by myself and talked to a wedding planner, because if I wanted to have my dream, I had to be the one planning it which was a huge problem for Sandra to let me plan anything. She will unpack a trunk I've already packed and is my verbal map when I drive. She tells me I'm wrong about putting dirty dishes in our dishwasher and asking people to bring a snack or dessert to a party.

"Tacky, and bring your own bottle? I can't believe you would ask people to bring their own drink when the party is at our house."

When she finally accepted the fact that I was planning a wedding with or without her support, she went with me to the Cliffs to talk to the wedding planner.

The next problem was that a wedding means holding hands and kissing in front of people, and Sandra won't even do that in a car or on a deserted beach in a foreign country for fear it might not be deserted. Next came discussing the guest list. I wanted to invite ladies from our two golf leagues.

Sandra argued, "You can't invite those ladies without inviting their husbands."

In a rare moment of contradicting her, I said "Watch me," and that's what I did. Next, I wanted to include people we knew well with no strangers and she wanted it even smaller. I wanted to invite some pickleball friends, and we compromised with the players she had met when they played on our home court.

I heard through Laurie Cross that Jack Timmons, a speech therapist from school, joked that he was going to crash our wedding if he didn't get an invitation. I was flattered, but that opened up an entirely new group of people I wanted to invite, so I argued with Sandra, "If someone would come to our funeral, I feel they deserve an invitation to our wedding," which finally became everyone's in.

When Sandra rolled her eyes every time I mentioned inviting someone, I answered, "Would they come to our funeral without their spouse?" Even though I had worn her down, every guest and suggestion was met with resistance.

"I suppose you want to sing," Sandra said.

I thought of several songs I sang at other weddings that I pictured singing to my own husband someday, but said, "No, not necessarily," while holding back tears.

I spent a lot of time organizing videos and photos of us and our family.

"Those are for funerals." She insisted with more rolled eyes.

I refused to cry or shout the responses running through my head. She really didn't want this wedding and I did, badly.

Our straight friend, Ellen Scott, said she wanted to get a minister's license and marry us and everything changed instantly. Our stress levels dropped, and she brought a calmness to us because we trusted her professionalism and wisdom, and knew she would be beautiful up there.

I wanted to use a recording of a song Sandra wrote to me when she was infatuated with me as our entrance. Sandra felt the sound quality wasn't good enough. Ellen had a recording of Train's 'Marry Me' in her phone. She played it for us and Sandra teared up. I never would have chosen a song about people at the beginning of their relationship, but I loved everything else about the song and since it made Sandra tear up, it was a no brainier to use it as our entrance song.

Ellen suggested using Sandra's original song on our way out as she knew people would be clapping and the sound quality wouldn't be a factor. She also knew of events besides funerals that used slide shows and felt the slide show would work. Our arguments didn't cease, but they lessened. We took our grandkids shopping for dressy, but not too dressy outfits and gave them a spending allowance so they had money left over.

I was getting my nails done the day before the wedding and my neighbor Peggy was there at the same time. She pointed to me and yelled, "That's the wedding I'm going to tomorrow!"

Over a dozen people looked at and congratulated me. Peggy left before me, and I sat there thinking, they all think I'm marrying a man.

After much consideration, I stood up to leave and said to everyone, "I'm getting married tomorrow on my 29th anniversary to a woman."

I couldn't believe the number of people who cheered and reached out to me saying, "Congratulations!"

I went outside and bawled my eyes out in the middle of the parking lot, totally out of control. I never made it to my car and couldn't stop sobbing. I had taken a chance and everyone in there was happy for me. One of the Vietnamese workers who caught the drift but not the specifics, said, "Happy Birthday!"

I still tear up every time I recollect that moment. It was hard and emotional for me to verbalize that I was gay and get such a positive unexpected response.

A year later I was at a party when one of the women who had been in the spa that day came over to me and reminded me of my bravery. She was one of the people who had reached out and enthusiastically congratulated me.

I wish I had taken her name so she could read how deeply her positive enthusiasm and acceptance still affects me and she wasn't the only one who reached out. The whole place was thrilled for me. I still tear up every time I read this and recollect that joyous emotional moment.

TWENTY SIX

The Wedding
Another Best Day of My Life

Close to a hundred family and close supportive friends came. We had two tables of golfing friends without their husbands, several pickleball friends, and many of my Martha Negus friends, and it felt like a reunion. My sister Phyllis flew in from Virginia with her gay son Don, who is one of my favorite people on the planet. Phyllis gave a heartwarming toast that reminded me how lucky I was to find Sandra. She ended with, "Remember, Mom and Dad taught us to never go to bed angry or without kissing goodnight."

Don was our patient sound tech, and he wore a Scottish kilt. People still talk about Justin's toast that had everyone laughing and crying. He stood beside me to walk me down the short aisle and when he took my hand, I struggled to hold back a sob that came out as a loud gasp. I have never made a sound like that in my life, and it was embarrassing, but the emotion of one of Sandra's sons taking my hand overtook me. Justin didn't know what to make of it and neither did I.

Justin asked if I was okay.

I was so much more than okay.

Jonathan walked Sandra down the aisle and Jason walked with his daughter Malia. Justin and I went behind them. It felt emotionally overwhelming seeing my bonus sons and Malia participating in our wedding. I had suggested to Sandra that Malia be a ring bearer, but Sandra wanted to keep everything simple and let Ellen give us the rings. It wasn't worth arguing over because I got my wedding at the Cliffs.

Another granddaughter Marley and her lesbian partner were the videographers and our friend Chev was happy to be the photographer. Every single person surrounding us was family or a close friend. Our other grandchildren Bailey, Ember, and Hayze also came with the added bonus of our oldest granddaughter Sascha who brought our precious great-granddaughter Scarlett.

Unfortunately fourteen-year-old Braeden had a good paying fishing job that day and regretted not being there. I asked if he thought his Nana and I getting married was kind of weird.

"I't's kinda cool," he said.

I felt ecstatic all day and was so in love with Sandra all over again. She looked like she was exuberant too. Any reservations about getting married disappeared on that day of laughter and smiles from friends and family congratulating us. It was the best day of my life, and I am glad we waited to get married with friends and family rather than some other state or country where it was legal.

I used a mic for my before the toast vows so everyone could hear. "Getting married after 29 years is quite different from getting married in those first couple glorious years of courtship. It was 29 years ago I was driving Sandra home at about midnight after our job when I stopped at Waller Park, determined to tell her I was gay. I was petrified of telling anybody in those days. I parked the car and I told Sandra I had something important to tell her and that I was scared to death she would reject me once she knew that about me. She kept coaxing me. "Barbara, there is nothing you could possibly say that could make me feel any differently about you."

"I am so worried, Sandra, that this is going to destroy our friendship." I whispered.

"Barbara, please tell me. I guarantee you there is nothing you could possibly say that could make me reject you. Nothing. I promise you."

Finally, with my hands trembling I choked out, "I'm gay."

Incredibly, Sandra turned toward me, took my hands and responded, "I don't know if I'm gay, but I know I love you," and we were so emotional there was electricity in our hands. That's not an expression. It was real electricity in our hands. Not only that, as we sat there holding hands and sharing our feelings toward each other we watched a full moon eclipse; more proof it was our special night. We didn't even kiss that night, but that was the night we vowed to each other we would be together forever - under an eclipsing moon.

Today's renewal of vows has been a reminder of how lucky I am to still have Sandra as my partner and now, unbelievably, my wife. It hasn't been 29 years of bliss. We've both been in pain and frustrated with each other and we've had to work really hard and even ask for outside help because loving someone deeply isn't enough. Sandra abhors going to counseling and airing our differences to anyone else, so agreeing to go once in a while at my request is proof of her commitment to me and our relationship. We have doubted that we would ever be able to marry, but we have never doubted that we would be there for each other in good times and in bad doing whatever it takes to respect and appreciate our love and devotion and commitment to each other, forever.

My Vows to Sandra:

I vow to remember that you are patient beyond measure with everyone and everything.

I vow to remember that you daily, without complaint, get up and help find my wallet, keys, credit card, phone, tickets, and any other number of items I lose daily. You are amazing.

I vow to remember that you are a master at fixing things, and you never quit unto it's fixed.

I vow to remember that you are a fabulous cook, and you don't want me in the kitchen.

I vow to remember that you are hostess extraordinaire, and you are always happy to have company.

I vow to remember that you are one of the kindest people on the planet and that was the first thing that attracted me to you.

I vow to remember that you are there for me and our friends when they get sick.

I vow to remember that you can remember every movie we've seen and who starred in, and every concert we've been to and the names of every person you meet.

I vow to remember that you are never rude about my total inability to recall movies, movie stars, concerts and the names of the many people we meet.

I vow to remember that the song 'She Don't Know She's Beautiful' was written with you in mind.

I vow to remember that you are a great help to 'Sound on Sound' on and off the job.

I vow to remember that you always have a neat desk, and you never complain about my messy desk and all the stuff spilling over it.

I vow to remember that you take primary responsibility for the upkeep of our beautiful home, and you don't mind sharing it with our many friends.

I vow to remember the only way I knew you graduated magna cum laude and suma cum laude from undergraduate school was because I helped you apply for a job and saw it on your diploma. For me, the only reason to graduate suma cum laude would be so I could yell it to the entire world, "Hey I did it! I graduated suma cum laude," but you tell no one and therein lies one of our biggest differences and hurdles in our relationship. You don't tell anybody about your accomplishments and I want to tell everyone, a difference that is not that important in the big picture.

I vow to continue to reread this and remind myself over and over again how lucky I am that I have had you by my side for these 29 incredible years, and that I will continue to have you by my side for the rest of our days.

I am so lucky, and I love you so very much.

I could barely hold back tears all day and felt grateful and so in love. I saw that Sandra was also overwhelmed several times when she wiped away tears of joy.

When we turned around after the ceremony everyone was on their feet clapping and whooping, giving us a heart warming standing ovation. Sandra grabbed my hand and kept holding it as we walked past the tables of our friends and family leaning toward us yelling, "Congratulations!" over and over again. I have no description of how exhilarating that moment was.

I often think about the many brave people who made this path possible for us and want to thank every one of them because I am so grateful that day came in my lifetime. That day and the day Sandra said she loved me, are the happiest days of life.

Do Sandra and I tell people we are married? It surprises me every time she introduces me as her wife. It's exciting to think that we are married, but we are still somewhat secretive. At a gig the other day a gentleman asked where my husband was, and I said my usual, "Not here."

I have to remind myself that half the people we meet think we're sinning freaks, but my God is not that shallow and prejudiced. I believe Sandra and I and our gay friends have as good a chance as anyone of getting to whatever Heaven is. If there is a God judging us I believe it's souls, not body parts that's on his checklist. My God is judging those making judgements in His name; the churches and the people who cause strife and pain.

Getting married got me thinking about the three women I got kicked out of Eastern Michigan University and I wondered if they are still together. Did they finish college somewhere else? Are they married to each other or to someone else? I still wonder why they didn't just talk to me instead of deciding to caress in front of me. What were they thinking? Someone asked me what would have happened in those days to guys and girls having relations in the rooms. They most likely would have been kicked out of the dorm, but they wouldn't have been expelled from college.

I still feel guilty for being so self-righteous and judgmental about gays and minorities. My mother changed too. She was living her advice to me as a child, "Don't judge people by their looks."

Now that I think about it, maybe dad appearing to me by walking through a door was his way of telling me I hadn't really shut him out. Maybe his message was that people can get through barriers and doors in this lifetime. Maybe it was a message about being open. My dad was agnostic and believed in a spiritual world, but questioned the Bible and organized religion. His walking through and reappearing from the closed door may have been a sign for me to spread the message that humanity needs to be more open minded. I believe he felt it important enough to appear to me and let me know that the spiritual world accepts me. "This is what is possible now, while you are living," he said.

When I shared this story with my friend Elisa she stopped me. "What door did you say he appeared from?"

"My closet door."

Elisa stared at me "Barbara, he told you he's only appearing to you once and he chose to disappear and then reappear to you from your closet door. Not just any wall or door, but your closet door! She kept repeating, "That was his message, Barbara. Come out of the closet."

A vast, open-minded, unbiased, loving, peaceful, spiritual world awaits all of us who are good.

TWENTY SEVEN

A Letter to Louise: A Biblical Affirmation of Homosexuality

Reproduced with permission from
WWW.GodMadeMeGay.com

By Bruce Lowe 2002

This piece was written by a man who read over 50 books trying to help his friend Louise. Louise told Bruce, "My brother hates God because God made him gay, and he knows he is going to hell, and so do I, for this is what the Bible says."

After years of study Bruce put the convictions he came to into ten statements that he believed Louise and other church families needed to understand about gays and lesbians. What follows are excerpts from Bruce's enlightening article. I recommend reading the entire article.

Homosexuality is an unchanged nature; it is not a lifestyle. Practically all behavioral scientists now accept this statement as fact.

Evidence that homosexuality is unchangeable includes 10,000 suicides each year of young homosexuals unwilling to face life with that orientation.

All people are created in the image of God. The homosexuality of gays and lesbians, created by God, is good, not evil.

Several passages in the Bible speak of same gender sex. In every instance, the Bible is talking about heterosexuals filled with lust, who become sex perverts. The Bible says nothing about homosexual people being sent to hell.

The burden imposed on homosexuals by society is a great evil. We should stand in revulsion against it, and do all we can to oppose prejudice, hatred, and the condemnation of a society that makes the homosexuals life more difficult.

The evidence is overwhelming that the United States is a society where there is a strong fear and a deep hatred of lesbians and gay men. There are over 100 murders of gays and lesbians recorded in the US each year.

A man walking in a wilderness area in Pennsylvania observed from a distance two women camped there, and they were holding hands. He walked back to his truck for his rifle. One of the women survived his shooting and wrote the book, *8 Bullets*.

A man asked where the nearest gay bar was. He said he wanted to shoot some queers. A few minutes later he did. Such things are happening everywhere in America and gays and lesbians live in constant anxiety about these kinds of hate crimes.

A Dallas judge gave a light sentence to a murderer explaining that the victim was only a homosexual.

Homosexuals experience prejudice by our churches. Like our society, our churches need to change. Kill a queer for Christ is a real bumper sticker.

Even after people end up in prison for crimes against homosexuals, few of them show any remorse for their crimes and believe they were justified and aligned with the religious traditions they came from. One prisoner stated that the pastor of his church said that homosexuals represented Satan and the devil, an argument every anti-Semite and racist has used with devastating consequences. When the funeral of Matt Shepard was held, a Baptist preacher from Kansas with sympathizers from several states were there marching in front of the funeral site with placard's reading, "God hates fags."

In the summer of 1998 fundamentalist Christian organizers, fearful of the consideration by some states of recognizing same gender marriage, spent hundreds of thousands of dollars on ads in major newspapers telling the nation that gays and lesbians are sick and sinful, they can and should be cured, and their rights and protection should be denied. They often piously say "We don't hate the sinner, only the sin," but they are lying.

Tim 4-1-4 "Everything created by God is good and would include homosexual marriage because God created homosexuality."

In 1975 a symposium on homosexuality at the annual meeting of the Christian Association agreed that promiscuity, fornication, and adultery should be regarded as sinful for both homosexuals and heterosexual persons.

A loving, committed, permanent relationship between two persons of the same sex was in an entirely different category and was not condemned in the scripture.

Full acceptance by society, including the blessings and legality of marriage should be extended to gays and lesbians in the same way it is to others.

One of the Vatican library's earliest liturgical documents is a marriage ceremony for two persons of the same sex. The document dates to the fourth century, if not earlier. Nine centuries before heterosexual marriage was declared a sacrament, the church liturgically celebrated same sex covenants.

TWENTY EIGHT

Who says homosexuality is a sin?
2021: God can't bless sin.

Pope Francis was overruled by the group of men at the Vatican who have the power to change what is and isn't a sin...Men, men who believe they are right, and no-one is going to change their mind. Not even the pope.

Growing up I never ate meat on Friday because it was a mortal sin, now it's just a sin during Lent. I think it became a sin as a way to help the fishing industry. Today not eating meat one day a week would help global warming, but people shouldn't have to feel like they will go to hell for eating meat. Being married to a non-Catholic is no longer a sin.

Too late for my sister.

Non-Catholics can now be buried in a Catholic cemetery.

I was taught that there is no Salvation outside the church, and that people who weren't Catholic were going to hell. Now there is salvation outside the church as, "A just, merciful God does not condemn people for being the wrong religion."

Hopefully, someday people will realize that a just and merciful God does not condemn homosexuality and throughout thousands of years on this planet, God has been our judge, not men. I find it interesting that many people pick and quote Bible verses that aren't just and merciful to keep proving they are right, rather than admit they are wrong.

According to the Catholic Church it is the willful disregard of a church discipline that can send people to hell forever. These "church disciplines" are human beings throughout the ages who believe they should decide who goes to heaven or hell.

In my world God is our judge, not people, and my God finds it sinful for people to claim that they decide who enters His kingdom. It's His kingdom. Not theirs.

According to their rules Catholics who purposely ate meat on Friday are burning in hell forever because they committed a mortal sin. It's the same situation for people with differing sexual orientations. They are not burning in hell because men say they are. God loves and respects us just like anyone else.

People are ignorant and biased, not God.

Jesus suffered on the cross for six hours; a cruel, unjust, and painful punishment for sure.

Hell is where people with different sexual identities are told by men they are destined to suffer forever in torture and fire Can you imagine how long King David and Jonathan have been burning in the flames of hell if this is true? They have forever to look forward to because David's love for Jonathan was greater than that of a woman.

Who says homosexuality is a sin? Men, not God.

Romans 13:1 was quoted March 21, 1933 to justify oppression and domination in the name of law and order. "The authorities that exist have been established by God."

In 2018 US Attorney General Jeff Sessions invoked it to justify separating children from their families.

Episcopal Bishop Sean Rowe stated, "We are Christians who support the dignity, safety, and equality of women and the LGBTQ people as an expression of our faith."

TWENTY NINE

The Lavender Scare
The History I didn't learn

Well before the congressional investigations of 1950, U.S. institutions had already developed an intricate and effective system of regulations, tactics, and personnel to uncover homosexuals that would become enforcement mechanisms during the Lavender Scare. This was related to a general expansion of the bureaucratic state during the late nineteenth century, with institutions that increasingly systematically categorized people as unfit or fit, including homosexuals in the unfit category along with people who were designated as "criminally insane" or "morally depraved", even though they did not consistently take regulatory action on this until later.

This is why our friend Dorothy Reed and her lesbian partner married men and the four of them lived together. They rode in the car as couples, walked into and out of their house as couples, attended business functions as couples, and went to dances as couples. The men got promoted after their marriages, and the women got accolades.

Almost 25,000 people love and agree with Bishop Tobin's ignorant self-righteous post, but he was just being a good Catholic priest.

Some say Pride events are harmful for children. Pedophiles are harmful to children. Bishop Tobin doesn't understand the difference between people with different sexual identities and pedophiles. Being a Catholic priest he should be aware of pedophiles, but unfortunately some priests are pedophiles and many are gay, but hopefully they aren't pedophiles.

What happens to children at a pride event?

I played an impressive Buglers Holiday on trumpet, and I followed it with live dance music that children and their parents danced to. There was a vocalist/guitarist, men dressed in drag who walked around and entertained. They didn't look much different from the cloaks a priest wears, but the music was louder and the drag queens wore make up. If that is harmful, why isn't a priest who wears a cloak harmful to children? As it turns out they often are, but what happens to children who come to pride events? They eat hotdogs or hamburgers with their two moms or two dads and other people's two moms or two dads, and maybe have ice cream for dessert.

I admit it feels good to attend an event where we are all proud, accepted, and celebrated, and people like Bishop Tobin and his followers aren't there. I try to picture my Catholic friends going to a pride event and hearing it's against their faith, then going to confession. "Bless me Father for I have sinned. I attended a pride event."

Unless you've been to one you can't appreciate how amusing Bishop Tobin's statement is, and those who agree with him do so because their level of maturity matches their level of education and intelligence which represents people still clinging to ignorance. The best part is that if you are educated and disagree with them they don't want you as a friend. They only want other uneducated friends. This book is printed in black and white or I'd be taking a red pen to correct all those errors that he felt passionate enough to post. I doubt he understands the difference between a pedophile and people with non-cisgender identities.

The hit song "Fly Me To The Moon" was written by Bart Howard, who lived with his male partner for 58 years.

Fly me to the moon and let me play among the stars
Let me see what spring is like on Jupiter and Mars
In other words hold my hand
In other words darling kiss me
Fill my heart with song
And let me sing forever more
You are all I long for
All I worship and adore
In other words please be true
In other words I love you
We've come a long way.

EPILOGUE

After my happy wedding day and public commitment to Sandra, I was inspired to write about my journey from extreme homophobia to marriage, revealing a secret I had buried for fifty years. Now, instead of continuing to bury my actions, I wondered about Jane. Whatever happened to her? Was she married? How did she explain being expelled from college to her parents? Was it on her records forever? Did my unforgivable actions ruin her life?

I could no longer bury my shameful actions and the guilt and shame welled up inside me all over again. I had to find her. I had so many questions, Was she even alive?

When people ask me what my book is about I avoid answering their logical question because once I tell them, their horror response is, "You got someone kicked out of college?" and the guilt and shame well up inside me all over again. I had to find her. I had so many questions, but mostly, was she OK? It wasn't easy finding her, but Sandra paid for a search website and finally found a person who was a possibility.

The information she found indicated they were married with four children and she had lost her husband several years ago. She was 72 years old and from Michigan, but there was no information about what schools she had attended or information that would gave me an assurance I had found the right person.

I wrote her and when I got no response after a week' s time I figured I probably had the right person because a "wrong" person probably would have let me know I should continue my search elsewhere. The other possibility was that I might have a wrong address, so I sent a second letter giving the person more information about myself and letting her know I wanted to find her. I sent it special delivery, so I would know if anyone was at that address.

ABOUT THE AUTHOR

I graduated from Eastern Michigan University with a BA in music education and a master's in special education. Then my prayers were answered when I miraculously got a job teaching physically disabled students in Lompoc, CA…an A+ job in an A+ location.

Currently I'm a professional musician who plays guitar, piano, trumpet and spoons and I record my own harmonies and I am always looking for gigs. My wife, Sandra and I were doing a dance in Palm Springs when a person from Celebrity Cruises hired us to be a dance band on the Millennium.

My book is a memoir about being raised Catholic and being a music director at my Catholic Church where I was taught that homosexuality is a mortal sin worthy of hell, forever. During my college years I got a friend expelled from college, for what I thought was homosexual activity. As she left the dorm she turned around and said to me, "You Are Really Going To Regret This Someday, Barbara." The only thing I regretted was her inviting me to her room on that fateful night.

Many years later I fell in love with a beautiful, brilliant, talented, caring and devoted mother who told me, "I don't know if I'm gay, but I know I love you." That was the greatest day of my life even though it began a life of secrecy and fear that we would be fired from our job as teachers. I assisted my disabled students in the bathroom and I was well aware that people confuse lesbians with pedophiles.

I feel God's love and I don't fear God's judgment of my relationship with Sandra at all. I believe in a God who is judging all of us, and my book illustrates how the Bible is filled with pick and choose contradictions. One of my students was a devout Catholic and in a wheelchair. There were two priests at her Catholic church. One of the priests was obviously uncomfortable with her, perhaps believing the Bible passages that said she was a sinner and she should not be allowed to approach the altar of God. The other priest loved her and treated her with respect and kindness. That is the choice we are all given. Are you going to choose to be like the first priest or the second priest?

Sandra and I got married on our 29th anniversary with over 100 friends and family joyously giving us a standing ovation. It was the most blessed day of my life. We travel, golf and made our driveway into the first pickleball court in Santa Maria.

I am very proud of this book because I believe it will bring peace to those who are continually being told they are sinners…well, we are sinners just like everyone else. I believe that even my God is grateful that I wrote this book. So I thank Him and my earthly helpful friends every day.

www.ingramcontent.com/pod-product-compliance
Lightning Source LLC
Chambersburg PA
CBHW070537030426
42337CB00016B/2237